GALVANIC: BEYOND THE REEF

TARAWA AND THE GILBERTS

November 1943

S. MATTHEW CHESER AND NICHOLAS ROLAND

Naval History and Heritage Command
Department of the Navy
Washington, DC
2020

Published by
Naval History and Heritage Command
805 Kidder Breese Street SE
Washington Navy Yard, DC 20374-5060
www.history.navy.mil

The authors would like to acknowledge the contributions of Randall Fortson, Richard Hulver, and Christopher Martin to the research, writing, and editing of this work.

Cover art: *Beachhead Scene, Marines at Tarawa*, drawing, charcoal and pastel on paper, by Kerr Eby, 1944 (NHHC 88-159-DG as a Gift of Abbott Laboratories)

CONTENTS

PROLOGUE: THE DEATH OF *SCULPIN*

At 1330, 19 November 1943, 154 miles north of Truk, the Japanese Pacific bastion in the Caroline Islands, the crew of *Sculpin* (SS-191) prepared for the violent end to her ninth and final patrol. Japanese destroyer *Yamagumo* had stalked the submerged vessel from the surface for nine hours. Several depth charge attacks had badly damaged the submarine. Twice she had surfaced only for her pursuer to force her below. With batteries exhausted and along with them any hope of escape, *Sculpin*'s commanding officer, Lieutenant Commander Fred Connaway, ordered his boat to surface and engage the enemy with her outmatched deck guns. Before climbing into the boat's conning tower, he ordered engineering officer Lieutenant George Brown to scuttle *Sculpin* if the upcoming battle turned against the Americans, as it likely would.

Sculpin roared to the surface and her crew manned their guns, opening fire as the Japanese warship patiently maneuvered aft of the submarine from 3,000 yards away. A shell from the second salvo of *Yamagumo's* 5-inch guns pierced the conning tower from starboard to port. Another round struck home above the forward torpedo room. *Yamagumo* closed in, machine guns raking the deck and killing several *Sculpin* sailors at their guns. The destroyer's gunfire killed four of the boat's officers outright, including Lieutenant Commander Connaway and his executive officer. Command passed to Lieutenant Brown, stationed below in the control room.

Preparing to scuttle the boat, Brown approached Captain John Cromwell, commodore of the three-boat wolfpack for which *Sculpin* served as flagship, and informed him of his orders. Cromwell agreed that Brown should scuttle *Sculpin* and order its crew to abandon ship, but "he stated he could not go with us because he was afraid that the information he possessed might be injurious to his shipmates at sea."[1] Lieutenant Brown rang up emergency speed, ordered abandon ship, waited one

1 Quote and information on *Sculpin*'s sinking from Carl LaVO, *Back from the Deep: The Strange Story of the Sister Subs Squalus and Sculpin* (Annapolis, MD: Naval Institute Press, 1994), 132, 124–34.

minute for the crew to escape, and opened the vents. As Brown and his officers and crew exited the hatches into open ocean and enemy fire, Cromwell remained below. From the water, Torpedoman Harry F. Toney watched *Sculpin's* radar mast ease below the waves, recalling later, "she made a beautiful dive."[2]

Commodore Cromwell sacrificed his life for fear that information that he possessed, if revealed under coercion, would seriously injure the Allied war effort and jeopardize American lives. For his actions, he posthumously received the Medal of Honor, the nation's highest military decoration.

What did Commodore Cromwell know that he judged more important than his own life? On 5 November 1943, Vice Admiral Charles Lockwood, Commander Submarine Forces, Pacific Fleet, met with Cromwell at Pearl Harbor. Lockwood outlined for Cromwell the plans for Operation Galvanic, the amphibious invasion of the Gilbert Islands scheduled for 20 November. Cromwell's wolfpack was part of a screening force of nine submarines assigned to monitor the nautical routes between Truk and the Gilberts and warn the Pacific Fleet of an anticipated Japanese Combined Fleet sortie meant to turn back the forthcoming assaults on the Japanese garrisons at Apamama, Makin, and Tarawa atolls. Vice Admiral Lockwood stressed the importance of secrecy, warning Cromwell to keep the information even from his own officers. Facing capture two weeks later, Cromwell chose to go down with *Sculpin* rather than risk revealing the immense operation already underway in the Central Pacific.[3]

2 Quote: Steven Trent Smith, "Why Captain John Cromwell Chose to Go Down With the Ship," *HistoryNet*, http://www.historynet.com/captain-john-cromwells-decision.htm, accessed 25 June 2019.

3 Lockwood's memoir of the war does not discuss signals intelligence, codenamed ULTRA, still classified at the time of publication. Cromwell also knew of the American breaking of the Japanese code and this knowledge contributed to his decision to go down with the ship. Charles A. Lockwood, *Sink 'Em All: Submarine Warfare in the Pacific* (New York: E. P. Dutton & Co., Inc., 1951), 132–33; LaVO, *Back from the Deep*, 124.

Galvanic was a joint operation under the United States Navy's Central Pacific Force to capture the Gilbert Islands, a Central Pacific chain straddling the equator. Its primary objectives were the capture of Apamama, Makin, and Tarawa atolls for future use as forward airfields to support subsequent operations in the Central Pacific. Approximately 200 ships and more than 35,000 soldiers and Marines would face around 5,600 Japanese combat and support troops. Despite the American preponderance of force, the Japanese would prove to be a tenacious foe.[4]

The operation is most remembered for the heavy losses suffered by the 2nd Marine Division in its heroic assault on Betio, the main island of Tarawa Atoll. The desperate fighting introduced Americans to the stark realities of amphibious warfare in the Pacific, prompting decades of questions related to the necessity of the battle and charges of negligence or incompetence on the part of its leaders. At the same time, Tarawa demonstrated that American combined operations could seize any Japanese position, no matter how strongly defended, a process that would play out repeatedly over the following 19 months.

Operation Galvanic was but the first step in an important new phase of the Pacific War, part of a far-flung naval operation shaped by the realities of a global war. Tasked with a limited operation and faced with stubborn enemy garrisons and potential counterattacks from powerful Japanese naval forces, Navy leaders struggled to balance the tactical need for massed firepower with operational requirements for speed and secrecy. Meanwhile, the largely untested state of amphibious doctrine, equipment,

---

4 Butaritari Atoll was the site of the Battle of Makin. Allied planners seem to have taken the name of another nearby atoll, Makin, to be the name of the Butaritari Atoll. Meanwhile the Americans referred to the specific island invaded as "Butaritari." In convention with American sources, this history will call Butaritari Atoll "Makin Atoll," and the island Butaritari. On forces involved, see Samuel Eliot Morison, *History of United States Naval Operations in World War II. Volume 7: Aleutians, Gilberts and Marshalls, June 1942–April 1944* (Boston: Little, Brown and Company, 1951), 114, 122; Joseph H. Alexander, *Across the Reef: The Marine Assault of Tarawa* (Washington, DC: Marine Corps Historical Center, 1993), 4.

and tactics against fortified targets added to the uncertainty of their task. Despite these uncertainties and difficulties, after only two months of planning and one week of combat, Fifth Amphibious Force wrested a fortified mid-ocean chain from enemy control. Difficult lessons learned in the process would benefit Allied operations in the Central Pacific and beyond for the rest of the war.

Tarawa Atoll from an altitude of 12,000 feet. Betio Island is the foreground (NHHC 80-G-83771).

STRATEGIC SETTING

By January 1943, Allied forces had stalled Axis advances and seized the initiative across the globe. At the Battle of the Coral Sea in May 1942, the Allies stemmed a Japanese advance on Port Moresby, New Guinea, and the Americans turned back an Imperial Japanese Navy attempt to seize Midway Atoll in June. Limited American counter-offensives in the Solomon Islands, under the Navy, and along the northeastern coast of New Guinea under the Army and General Douglas MacArthur, sought to secure Allied lines of communication with Australia and ultimately to capture the Japanese bastion at Rabaul on the island of New Britain. Anglo-American forces were advancing in North Africa and a Soviet counteroffensive surrounded the German Sixth Army at Stalingrad and blocked Axis breakthrough attempts.

Against this backdrop, Anglo-American military and political leaders met beginning 14 January at the Casablanca Conference in recently liberated French Morocco, intending to establish Allied military objectives for 1943. Even before entering the war, the United States had committed to an Allied policy of defeating Germany before undertaking major offensive actions against Japan. By late 1942, with Japan on the defensive and the products of American shipyards and dry docks swelling the American fleet, Chief of Naval Operations and Commander-in-Chief, United States Fleet Admiral Ernest King pushed the American Joint Chiefs of Staff (JCS) for an official policy of constant pressure on Japan. By the time of the Casablanca Conference, the JCS were prepared to lobby for an aggressive approach in the Pacific.[5]

With the fall of Rabaul deemed imminent, the conference considered next steps in the Pacific. In contrast to their American counterparts, British members of the Combined Chiefs of Staff (CCS) entered the conference arguing for a continuation of an overall defensive posture in the Pacific. They desired continued American support for a "Europe-first" strategy and advocated only for limited counter-offensives against Rabaul and

5 Grace Person Hayes, *The History of the Joint Chiefs of Staff in World War II: The War Against Japan* (Annapolis, MD: Naval Institute Press, 1982), 260–64.

in Burma, although their enthusiasm for the latter operation was weak. The Americans staunchly maintained their desire for ambitious offensive operations against Japan.[6]

The vital flow of raw materials from the Japanese-held Dutch East Indies was crucial to Japan's war effort and the islands appeared to be a natural objective for those favoring an expanded offensive in the Pacific. At Casablanca, Admiral King argued instead for seizure of the Philippines, gaining control of the sea-lanes between the East Indies and Japan and cutting the Japanese off from crucial supplies of oil, tin, and rubber. Echoing decades of United States naval strategy, King next asserted that the preferred route to the Philippines was through the Central Pacific, and he maintained that the fall of Rabaul would free resources in the Pacific theater for an operation against the Marshalls and Carolines without risking operations in Europe. A Central Pacific operation would also fill an interval of inactivity between the end of the Rabaul offensive and planned operations in Burma, allowing the Allies to retain the strategic initiative. Army Chief of Staff General George C. Marshall finally allayed British concerns with a pledge that a Central Pacific campaign would draw only from "the resources available in the theater." The CCS endorsed the concept of the operation, so long as it did not interfere with operations against Germany and, "if time and resources allow[ed]," without harming operations in Burma. This was hardly a full sanctioning of American views, but it was progress from the "minimum essential" effort officially granted to the Pacific by Allied planners up to that time.[7]

---

6 Ibid., 279–91; *Casablanca Conference, January 1943: Joint Chiefs of Staff Minutes of Meetings* (Washington, DC: Office of the Combined Chiefs of Staff, 1943), 23–24, 55–56, 65; David Rigby, *Allied Master Strategists: The Combined Chiefs of Staff in World War II* (Annapolis, MD: Naval Institute Press, 2012), 72–75.

7 Edward S. Miller, *War Plan Orange: The U.S. Strategy to Defeat Japan, 1897–1945* (Annapolis, MD: Naval Institute Press, 1991), 92–98, 116–21, 192, 207, 237–37; Philip A. Crowl and Edmund G. Love, *United States Army in World War II. The War in the Pacific: Seizure of the Gilberts and Marshalls* (Washington, DC: Department of the Army, 1955), 7–10; Hayes, *Joint Chiefs of Staff*, 290–291.

With tentative approval of the concept secured, Admiral King and his staff continued to push for a commitment to the Marshalls-Carolines-Marianas axis of advance. Their efforts in the spring of 1943 finally garnered explicit approval for the proposed offensive. At the Anglo-American Trident conference in Washington, DC, from 12 to 25 May, the CCS approved an American plan calling for a general offensive in the Pacific. British concerns over the United States' ambitious plans for the theater had diminished by this time due to the buildup of American military power in 1943, the successes achieved thus far with limited forces in the Southwest Pacific, and the shifting of momentum toward the Allies in the Battle of the Atlantic. By the end of the Trident conference, the Allies were committed to a plan that identified multiple offensive objectives in the Pacific, shifting primacy from the Southwest Pacific and designating the Central Pacific offensive the main effort in the theater of operations.[8] They scheduled the first stage of the Central Pacific drive for November 1943.[9]

THE JAPANESE IN THE CENTRAL PACIFIC

During World War I, Japan, an ally of the Entente powers, had captured German Pacific territories including the northern Marianas, Caroline, and Marshall Islands. Japan acquired the former German possessions in 1920 as a League of Nations mandate. Following Japan's departure from the league in 1933, they continued to administer and develop these territories. The Japanese began to militarize the mandated islands even before their withdrawal in 1936 from the Washington Naval Treaty (1922), which prohibited—with the notable exception of Hawaii —new military infrastructure on the Pacific islands administered by Great Britain, Japan, and the United States. In the weeks after the attack on Pearl Harbor, Japan seized the American possessions of Guam in the Marianas Islands and

8 Rigby, *Allied Master Strategists*, 71–78; Crowl and Love, *Seizure of the Gilberts and Marshalls*, 13.

9 Thomas B. Buell, *The Quiet Warrior: A Biography of Admiral Raymond A. Spruance* (Annapolis, MD: Naval Institute Press, 1987), 180.

War Plan Orange

The United States Army and Navy periodically collaborated on war contingency plans for future conflicts with color-coded adversaries beginning in the early 1900s. For example, Germany was coded Black, Russia was designated Purple, and Japan was referred to as Orange.[1] The Navy took the lead in planning for war in the Pacific, developing a rudimentary version of Plan Orange by 1906 and identifying Japan as the likeliest future opponent as early as 1919.[2] Though its details varied in several iterations prior to 1941, Plan Orange envisioned an initial period of defensive operations in reaction to a Japanese attack, followed by an island-hopping campaign across the Central Pacific to the Philippines, culminating in a naval blockade and aerial bombardment campaign that would strangle the Japanese economy and end the war.[3] Between 1939 and 1941, the interservice Joint Planning Committee developed a new series of plans codenamed "Rainbow" to reflect the apparent likelihood of a coalition war against a multinational Axis.[4] Approved by President Franklin D. Roosevelt in 1941, Rainbow Five, with the United States allied with Britain and France and the defeat of Germany as the first priority, superseded Plan Orange and called for a prolonged defensive war in the Pacific.[5] Nonetheless, many of the concepts of Plan Orange remained imprinted in the thinking of Navy leaders. The Navy's insistence on initiating the Central Pacific Drive in 1943 reflected decades of American naval strategy and proved to be the decisive campaign of the war.

1 James F. Dunnigan and Albert A. Nofi, *The Pacific War Encyclopedia, Vol. 2* (New York: Facts on File 1998), 647.

2 Edward S. Miller, *War Plan Orange: The U.S. Strategy to Defeat Japan, 1897–1945* (Annapolis, MD: Naval Institute Press, 1991), 21; George W. Baer, *One Hundred Years of Sea Power: The U.S. Navy, 1890–1990* (Stanford, CA: Stanford University Press, 1994), 90.

3 Miller, *War Plan Orange*, 4.

4 Ibid., 213–15.

5 Ibid., 270–71.

Wake Island. The undefended British colonies of the Gilbert Islands, to the southeast of the Marshalls, also fell to the Japanese. These campaigns were complete by 24 December 1941. Following these conquests, the Japanese exercised effective control over the entirety of Micronesia.[10]

The most important Japanese base in the Central Pacific was the island of Truk in the Carolines. The Imperial Japanese Navy's Combined Fleet

10 Morison, *Aleutians, Gilberts and Marshalls*, 70–71, 74; *Limitation of Naval Armament (Five-Power Treaty or Washington Treaty)*, 6 February 1922, https://www.loc.gov/law/help/us-treaties/bevans/m-ust000002-0351.pdf, accessed 24 September 2019; Crowl and Love, *Seizure of the Gilberts and Marshalls*, 60–61.

under Admiral Mineichi Koga, the service's main fighting force, rested at anchor in the Truk lagoon for much of 1943. Despite carrier losses at Midway, it remained formidable and included the super-battleships *Yamato* and *Musashi*. By September 1943, Truk boasted 6 battleships, 3 carriers, 11 heavy cruisers, 3 light cruisers, and a large number of destroyers.[11] The Japanese Fourth Fleet, a much smaller organization responsible for the South Pacific Mandates, had a forward anchorage at Kwajalein in the Marshalls and administered many of the garrisons in the islands.[12]

Japanese strategy revolved around luring American naval forces into a climactic, decisive sea battle. The concept guiding Japanese defenses was *Yogeki sakusen*, translated as "waylaying counterattack." Island garrisons defending the perimeter of Japanese territory were to act as a sort of trip wire, holding out and occupying invasion forces long enough so that land-based air, submarines, and the Combined Fleet could concentrate, counterattack, and destroy the American fleet.[13] Articulated in May 1942 as "Z Operation," the plan had antecedents in Japanese strategic thinking in the late 1930s and emphasized the defense of a north-south line formed by the Aleutians, Wake Island, the Gilberts and Marshalls, Nauru, Ocean (Banaba) Island, and the Bismarcks. This plan increased the importance of the Gilberts. It also emphasized a tenacious defensive posture, with local commanders responsible for destruction of the invading U.S. forces at the waterline and immediate counterattacks against any American beachheads.[14] The *Hei* No. 3 operation plan specifically outlined Admiral Koga's response to an Allied invasion of the Gilberts. The Japanese would move the Combined Fleet, aircraft, submarines, and reinforcements into the islands upon detecting an invasion force. If the garrisons could hold

---

11 Crowl and Love, *Seizure of the Gilberts and Marshalls*, 68.

12 Ibid., 60–61.

13 Joseph H. Alexander, *Utmost Savagery: The Three Days of Tarawa* (Annapolis, MD: Naval Institute Press, 1995), 19–20.

14 David C. Evans and Mark R. Peattie, *Kaigun: Strategy, Tactics, and Technology in the Imperial Japanese Navy, 1887–1941* (Annapolis, MD: Naval Institute Press, 1997), 464–67, 91–92; Crowl and Love, *Seizure of the Gilberts and Marshalls*, 65.

out for three to seven days, the Combined Fleet would attempt to engage the fixed invasion fleet and achieve a decisive victory at sea.[15]

CONCEIVING GALVANIC

American planning identified the Marshall Islands as the natural first target of a Central Pacific offensive. Standing astride lines of communication between Hawaii and the Philippines, the archipelago contained eight operational Japanese airbases.[16] If captured, the Marshalls would allow Allied land-based aircraft to join the campaign against Japanese lines of communication, protect and extend Allied lines of communication, and serve as a launching point for further operations in Micronesia.[17]

The Marshalls, however, provided planners with some significant problems. First, to capture or otherwise neutralize the large number of fortified bases in the island group would require a sizeable commitment of men and resources. By CCS agreement, these forces were to come from those already allocated to the Pacific. Initial plans called for two divisions of battle-tested amphibious troops along with vessels for transport and supply. The logical units to deploy were the 1st and 2nd Marine Divisions, already serving under MacArthur in the Southwest and South Pacific. Vice Admiral William F. "Bull" Halsey's transports and supply ships in the South Pacific would also support the Central Pacific operation. MacArthur and his allies in the War Department bristled at the suggestion of depriving his command of its amphibious divisions and shipping, which would halt his advance and force him to take the defensive.[18]

Beside the question of forces available, intelligence on the Marshalls was scarce—in the words of Navy historian Samuel Eliot Morison, Japan had "dropped a thick curtain of secrecy around" its Micronesian possessions after withdrawing from the League of Nations in 1933.[19] The

15 Alexander, *Utmost Savagery*, 39.

16 Ibid., 15.

17 Crowl and Love, *Seizure of the Gilberts and Marshalls*, 15.

18 Ibid., 20–21.

19 Morison, *Aleutians, Gilberts and Marshalls*, 71.

Americans could not be sure what fortifications, units, and hydrographic conditions they would face in the Marshalls, and such answers required high-quality reconnaissance. The Marshalls, however, were outside of the effective range of American aerial reconnaissance.[20]

These difficulties prompted planners to look southeast to the Gilbert Islands. Consisting of 16 islands and atolls straddling the equator between longitudes 173 and 175 degrees, the Gilberts provided remedies for the most serious flaws of the Marshalls. The Japanese had only recently occupied these British possessions. Consequently, they were less fortified and developed than the Marshalls. The Joint Staff Planners estimated that a smaller attacking force of one division and one regimental combat team could secure the islands, allowing offensive operations to continue in other areas of the Pacific. The island chain was also within range of U.S. Seventh Air Force bombers stationed on Funafuti in the Ellice Islands and Canton in the Phoenix Islands, which could provide air support and aerial reconnaissance.[21] Capture of the Gilbert archipelago would shorten and secure lines of communications to Australia and New Zealand and allow for mutual support between the South Pacific and Central Pacific theaters. The islands' occupation would block the last possible Japanese route of advance into Allied waters, a potential assault on Samoa and Fiji, and the Gilberts would provide a forward base essential for the subsequent capture of the Marshalls.[22] Finally, the operation would serve as an invaluable test of amphibious doctrine against coral atolls before attacking the heavily defended Marshalls.

Early advocacy for this course of action came from Vice Admiral Raymond A. Spruance, chief of staff to Admiral Chester W. Nimitz, Commander-in-Chief, Pacific Ocean Areas. Nimitz concurred, and in

---

20 Alexander, *Utmost Savagery*, 15–16.

21 Crowl and Love, *Seizure of the Gilberts and Marshalls*, 39, 52–53.

22 Henry I. Shaw Jr., Bernard C. Nalty, and Edwin T. Turnbladh, *History of U.S. Marine Corps Operations in World War II, Volume 3: Central Pacific Drive* (Washington, DC: Historical Branch, U.S. Marine Corps, 1966), 13.

turn sent his recommendations to the Joint Chiefs of Staff.[23] On 20 July 1943, the JCS agreed to the capture of the Gilberts and the outlying island of Nauru.[24] The JCS ordered Nimitz to organize and train forces to "capture, occupy, defend, and develop bases" on the targets by 15 November 1943, and code-named the operation Galvanic.[25]

JAPANESE CONTROL OF THE GILBERTS

The Gilberts, while less forbidding than the Marshalls, would not be an easy objective. Aside from establishing a seaplane base at Makin, the Japanese largely neglected the Gilberts until American air and amphibious raids struck the islands in February and August 1942. The raids accomplished little of strategic value, but prompted the Japanese to reinforce the Gilberts. The Japanese increased the Makin garrison, depleted by the raid, on 30 August, and occupied Apamama Atoll on 31 August. The Yokosuka 6th *Rikusentai*, or Special Naval Landing Force, with 1,509 men, landed at Tarawa Atoll on 15 September, sending detachments to Makin and Apamama. Nearby, the Japanese captured the phosphate islands of Nauru and Ocean on 25–26 August.[26]

The Japanese also fortified the archipelago. In October 1942, Major Dempachi Kondo of Imperial General Headquarters singled out Tarawa Atoll as crucial for the defense of the Gilberts. He recommended building an airfield on Betio, the main island of the atoll, at the same time reinforcing and fortifying the island. By November 1942, the Japanese began building the recommended airfield, which was operational by March 1943 and, in late December 1942, they began to transform Tarawa into a formidable island stronghold. Japanese forces also dug in on Butaritari and Nauru, building a small airstrip on the latter.[27]

23 Buell, *Quiet Warrior*, 180–182.

24 Ibid., 182; Crowl and Love, *Seizure of the Gilberts and Marshalls*, 23.

25 Crowl and Love, *Seizure of the Gilberts and Marshalls*, 23, 25.

26 Ibid., 60–63.

27 Alexander, *Utmost Savagery*, 31–33.

In July 1943, Rear Admiral Kenji Shibasaki arrived on Betio. The energetic commander raised the garrison's morale, enhanced its training, and oversaw the engineers' activities. He molded a tenacious and skilled fighting force and hardened its position against attack.[28] Fortifications on the island proliferated, designed in accordance with Z Operation's guidance to prevent or defeat enemy beachheads. Mutually supporting positions, including concrete bunkers and bomb-proof shelters, coral and coconut-log firing positions, trenches, and prefabricated metal pillboxes, studded the island by D-day. A six-foot-tall coconut-log seawall fringed large portions of the shoreline. Double-apron barbed wire, anti-boat tetrahedrons made of steel beams, and sea mines denied most approaches to the shoreline, channeling invading boats into areas covered by guns. Betio bristled with heavy weaponry: seven tanks with 37-mm guns; four 140-mm, four 127-mm, and six 80-mm guns; ten 75-mm mountain howitzers; six 70-mm howitzers; eight 70-mm dual-purpose single mounts; nine 37-mm field guns; twenty-seven 13-mm single mounts; four 13-mm double mounts; and four 8-inch naval rifles.[29] The island had 58 guns firing 37-mm ammunition or larger in an area roughly one third the size of New York's Central Park.[30]

In contrast to Tarawa, a lieutenant (j.g.), Seizō Ishikawa, commanded at Makin. Defenses on Butaritari, lying at the southern end of the atoll, aimed to protect the seaplane base on the lagoon at the island's center. This conceded the landing beaches on the east and west ends of the long, T-shaped coral island. Bordering the defended areas were two roughly parallel systems of anti-tank obstacles built across the island. Both consisted of a wide ditch, five or six feet deep, covered by small arms and anti-tank positions. Makin had no gun over 80-mm and a limited number of anti-aircraft and anti-tank guns and field artillery.[31]

28 Ibid., 40–41.

29 Alexander, *Across the Reef*, 3.

30 Crowl and Love, *Seizure of the Gilberts and Marshalls*, 74.

31 Ibid., 71–73.

The Japanese had about 4,800 men at Tarawa on D-day, including 1,497 men of the Sasebo 7th Special Naval Landing Force, the Japanese equivalent to the Marines, and 1,122 combat troops in the 3rd Special Base Force.[32] The remainder were construction battalions, composed partially of conscripted Korean laborers, with rudimentary military training. In total, there were approximately 3,000 effective combat troops concentrated on Betio, with small detachments on the atoll's other islands. Makin hosted 798 men, with between 300 and 400 combat troops consisting of a detachment of *Rikusentai* and 100 aviation personnel. Japanese construction personnel were armed and prepared to fight on both islands.[33] A token observation force guarded the final Galvanic objective, Apamama, which was not fortified.[34]

LEADERSHIP AND PERSONNEL

To initiate the Navy's Central Pacific offensive, Nimitz chose Spruance as Commander, Central Pacific Force.[35] Spruance was already a household name due to his actions while commanding Task Force (TF) 16 at the Battle of Midway. Though the press and rivals in the Navy had pilloried Spruance for failing to pursue the Japanese fleet following the battle, Nimitz greatly approved of his performance and intelligence reports later vindicated Spruance's actions. Described by his biographer as "the Quiet Warrior," he possessed a brilliant mind and was even-tempered and restrained. As a leader, he preferred to delegate, disliked and avoided conflict, and let subordinates hammer out details. Since Spruance had no

32 Ibid., 73.

33 Ibid., 71–73.

34 Shaw, Nalty, and Turnbladh, *Central Pacific Drive*, 32, 100–101.

35 "The ships under Spruance's command were designated the Fifth Fleet. The forces under his command—Army, Navy, and Marine Corps—were designated the Central Pacific Force. In 1944, the latter title was dropped, and his command was called simply the 'Fifth Fleet.'" Buell, *Quiet Warrior*, 188n1.

amphibious experience, Galvanic would require the admiral to rely heavily on his subordinates.[36]

The "Quiet Warrior," Admiral Raymond A. Spruance, Commander, Central Pacific Force, U.S. Pacific Fleet, taken 23 April 1944 (NHHC 80-G-225341.

Unsurprisingly, Spruance turned to recognized experts in amphibious warfare as his principal subordinates. In July, he chose Rear Admiral Richmond Kelly Turner to command the amphibious task forces, including transports, landing craft, escorts, and naval gunfire support ships. Soon to be designated the Fifth Amphibious Force, Turner's command came to be nicknamed "V Phib." Turner earlier served as Bull Halsey's

36 Buell, *The Quiet Warrior*, xiii–xv, xxix.

Rear Admiral Richmond K. Turner

Rear Admiral Richmond Kelly Turner was the foremost amphibious commander in the U.S. Navy during World War II. Known as "Terrible Turner," he was a hard-driving authoritarian who demanded excellence from his subordinates. A native of California and a Naval Academy Class of 1908 graduate, Turner's early service included a variety of sea duty and staff assignments. Flight qualification in 1927 seems to have benefited his career trajectory, and he thereafter commanded several aviation squadrons, worked as an aviation planner, advised the United States delegation at the failed World Disarmament Conference in 1932, and served as the executive officer on *Saratoga* (CV-3) in 1933–34.[1]

Turner's promotion to rear admiral came in 1941, while he served as director of the Navy's War Plans Division in Washington, DC. He was assistant chief of staff to Admiral Ernest King between December 1941 and June 1942, and then proceeded to the Pacific to take command of the amphibious elements of Bull Halsey's South Pacific Force.[2] Turner first gained experience as an amphibious force commander during the Solomon Islands campaign, especially through the complex operations in New Georgia.[3]

By the conclusion of Galvanic, Turner was the Navy's undisputed flag officer expert on amphibious warfare. He would go on to command amphibious operations to seize the Marshalls, Saipan, Tinian, Guam, Iwo Jima, and Okinawa. Turner was promoted to vice admiral in April 1945 in the midst of the Okinawa fighting and to admiral the next month. He then began to plan for the Allied assault on the Japanese Home Island of Kyushu,

1 Dunnigan and Nofi, *The Pacific War Encyclopedia, Vol. 2,* 618; "Admiral Richmond K. Turner, USN (1885–1961)," https://www.history.navy.mil/content/history/nhhc/our-collections/photography/us-people/t/turner-richmond-k.html, accessed 13 September 2019.

2 "Admiral Richmond K. Turner."

3 Morison, *Breaking the Bismarcks Barrier,* 224.

amphibious commander in the Solomons. Turner's fitness report from the campaign described him aptly: "A brilliant officer with fine character. Is somewhat intolerant in dealing with others."[37] Spruance selected the abrasive Major General Holland "Howlin' Mad" Smith, USMC, to command the Fifth Amphibious Corps (VAC), created on 4 September 1943. A pioneer of amphibious warfare, and an important voice shaping War Plan Orange, Smith spent much of the interwar years developing

37 George C. Dyer, *The Amphibians Came to Conquer, Volume 2* (Washington, DC: Government Printing Office, 1972), 599.

codenamed Operation Olympic. Fortunately, the invasion of Japan never occurred.[4] Representative Carl Vinson (D–GA), chairman of the House Naval Affairs Committee, summarized Turner's war record in a message sent 17 August 1945: "Our successes on land have been in a large measure due to your skill, courage and tenacity of purpose in conducting these operations. Your devotion to duty has been an inspiration to all of us."[5]

Rear Admiral Richmond K. Turner aboard ship. By the conclusion of Galvanic, Turner was the Navy's undisputed flag officer expert on amphibious warfare (NHHC 80-G-216636).

4 Dunnigan and Nofi, *The Pacific War Encyclopedia, Vol. 2*, 618; Dyer, *The Amphibians Came to Conquer*, 1107–10.

5 Dyer, *The Amphibians Came to Conquer*, 1113–14.

amphibious doctrine and equipment.[38] Smith had trained many of the Army and Marine amphibious units then fighting in the Pacific and the Mediterranean. As commander of VAC, he would lead all expeditionary troops. Spruance tapped Rear Admiral Charles A. Pownall to command carrier forces in the operation, Task Force 50, based on seniority.[39]

38 Anne C. Venzon, *From Whaleboats to Amphibious Warfare: Lt. Gen. "Howling Mad" Smith and the U.S. Marine Corps* (Westport, CT: Praeger, 2003), 50.

39 Clark G. Reynolds, *Admiral John H. Towers: The Struggle for Naval Air Supremacy* (Annapolis, MD: Naval Institute Press, 1991), 429.

Amphibious warfare pioneer Major General Holland M. Smith (left) with Major General Ralph J. Mitchell at Rear Admiral Osborne B. Hardison's headquarters in the South Pacific, 16 June 1943 (NHHC NH 58134).

The commanders and staffs of the infantry divisions also played an important role in planning and executing the campaign. When the joint planners presented the concept for Galvanic in July, they recommended the 2nd Marine Division be employed in the operation. It was a battle-tested, amphibious-trained division, currently recuperating in New Zealand after a grueling campaign in the malarial jungles of the Solomons. The JCS and

Nimitz were able to pry the division away from MacArthur and Halsey for the Gilberts operation. The division's commander was Major General Julian C. Smith, an affable man and a capable planner and tactician. Appeasing MacArthur, the 1st Marine Division was left in Australia and, in its place, the 27th Infantry Division was offered by the War Department in late July. The 27th was an untested New York National Guard unit. After mobilizing for federal service in 1940, they had performed garrison duty in California and Hawaii. Major General Ralph C. Smith, a keen tactician who had studied and lectured at the French *École de guerre*, commanded the division.[40]

INITIAL PLANNING FOR GALVANIC

The JCS named the Gilberts and the island of Nauru as Nimitz's objectives, but did not specify objectives within the archipelago. Tarawa Atoll was an essential target, as its main island of Betio held the only operational airfield in the Gilberts. Nimitz's orders specifically identified Nauru as another target.[41] Located 380 miles west of Tarawa, outside of the Gilberts group, Nimitz's planners favored the island due to its completed airfield and its ability to broaden the front of the Allied amphibious advance.[42] American planners also chose Apamama, believed to be virtually undefended, because of its great potential as an air base site and due to its large, calm lagoon judged to have "good holding ground" for a forward anchorage.[43] Spruance assigned the capture of Tarawa and Apamama to the 2nd Marine Division, and Nauru to the 27th Infantry Division.

Staffs on all levels conducted concurrent planning for Galvanic at Oahu, Territory of Hawaii, and Wellington, New Zealand, ironing out their differences in a series of conferences. One thing on which most of these diverse voices could agree was the unsuitability of Nauru as a target. Holland Smith warned of the tactical nightmare posed by the island's

40 Shaw, Nalty, and Turnbladh, *Central Pacific Drive*, 26.

41 Hayes, *The History of the Joint Chiefs of Staff in World War II*, 426.

42 Reynolds, *Admiral John H. Towers*, 435–36.

43 Dyer, *The Amphibians Came to Conquer*, 632.

extreme topography—cliffs rising out of the ocean, jagged phosphate quarries hewn out of the rock, and a surrounding reef that threatened to disrupt landing operations. Spruance, Turner, Holland Smith, and Vice Admiral John H. Towers, Commander Air Force, Pacific Fleet, also fretted about the substantial distance between Tarawa and Nauru. Simultaneous operations would split the forces and their escorts, making them vulnerable to Japanese naval counterattack. They deemed Nauru's seizure unnecessary, arguing that bombardment could neutralize the island and that it could then be isolated for the remainder of the war.[44]

Holland Smith prepared a revised estimate of the situation, endorsed by Turner and Spruance, suggesting Makin Atoll as a suitable replacement. The estimate expected light defenses and noted that the island was flat, providing an ideal site for a future airfield. It was also the atoll closest to the Marshalls and lay only 136 miles from Tarawa. Spruance presented Smith's argument, endorsed by Turner, to Nimitz and King while the two conferred in Pearl Harbor on 24 September.[45] King agreed, and the JCS approved the substitution of Makin for Nauru on 5 October. The 27th Infantry Division scrapped previous planning and VAC began drafting plans for the division's reinforced 165th Infantry Regiment (hereafter 165th RCT—Regimental Combat Team) to take the island of Butaritari in Makin Atoll.

The replacement of Nauru underscores a central assumption of Galvanic planning: that the Imperial Japanese Combined Fleet was willing and able to sortie from Truk and attack the Central Pacific Force. Combatant ships sacrifice maneuverability to screen troop transports and support an amphibious assault, and are especially vulnerable to attack from air and sea during a landing operation. Prior amphibious landings in the Mediterranean and the South Pacific had lost ships to air, surface, and

44 Reynolds, *Admiral John H. Towers*, 436.

45 Shaw, Nalty, and Turnbladh, *Central Pacific Drive*, 27–28; Morison, *Aleutians, Gilberts and Marshalls*, 84–85.

submarine attack. A Japanese torpedo plane had helped sink Turner's own flagship, *McCawley* (AP-10), at the landing at Rendova in June 1943.[46]

Major General Julian C. Smith, taken on 28 November 1943, possibly on Tarawa, by the 2nd Marine Division. Smith was an affable man and a capable planner and tactician (NHHC USMC 67699).

46 Alexander, *Utmost Savagery*, 78; "*McCawley* II (AP-10)," *Dictionary of American Naval Fighting Ships* (hereafter DANFS), https://www.history.navy.mil/research/histories/ship-histories/danfs/m/mccawley-ii.html, accessed 17 September 2019.

Galvanic's multiple objectives amplified the danger, dispersing forces and risking defeat in detail. Signals intelligence gathered in a series of air raids in September and October supported these fears. When a three-carrier task force under Rear Admiral Charles A. Pownall struck Tarawa and Makin on 18–19 September, radio direction finders detected the Japanese Combined Fleet steaming from Truk to the Marshalls. After TF 14 under Rear Admiral Alfred Montgomery hit Wake Island on 5–6 October, U.S. units detected the fleet in the Marshalls again.[47] Planners estimated that the enemy could launch a combined air and submarine attack within three days of sighting the American ships.[48] Secrecy and speed were imperative to accomplish the landings before the Japanese could interfere. If U.S. forces could quickly capture the targeted atolls, Spruance's fleet would dwarf any Japanese counterattack and could perhaps win a decisive victory at sea. Nimitz's orders to Spruance were clear: "Get the hell in, and get the hell out."[49]

INTELLIGENCE

Galvanic posed an intelligence problem for Central Pacific Force. The nature of amphibious warfare rendered difficult traditional methods of gathering combat intelligence, including interrogation of prisoners and capturing documents. Though the Marine raiders had captured some documents on Makin in August 1942, in the intervening year the situation on the ground had changed drastically. Human intelligence was not available to fill the void. In a crackdown following the raid, the Japanese killed or captured many New Zealander and British coast watchers and sympathizers while confiscating or destroying wireless equipment.[50] Oceanographic data, including accurate tide tables and reef locations, were especially crucial to planning a successful amphibious assault, but

47 Dyer, *The Amphibians Came to Conquer*, 638–39.

48 Shaw, Nalty, and Turnbladh, *Central Pacific Drive*, 37.

49 Alexander, *Utmost Savagery*, 78.

50 Crowl and Love, *Seizure of the Gilberts and Marshalls*, 63–64.

U.S. planners found that the maps, soundings, and nautical data at their disposal were unreliable.[51]

The American staffs turned to several sources to fill the void. Signals intelligence, using cracked Japanese code, provided important but incomplete information on enemy strength and dispositions. As a result, aerial photography and reconnaissance proved crucial to estimating enemy strength in the Gilberts. To obtain more bases for reconnaissance and air support, American forces occupied the Ellice atolls of Nukufetau and Nanumea in August, and reoccupied the U.S. possession of Baker Island, 700 miles east of Tarawa, in early September. Army Air Forces engineers constructed an airfield on Baker by 11 September, and airfields on the other islands were ready in October.[52]

Army and Navy Consolidated B-24 Liberator bombers from Baker, Nukufetau, and Nanumea now joined those from Funafuti and Canton in bombing and photographing Tarawa, Makin, and the southern Marshalls. *Lexington*'s (CV-16) aircraft in Pownall's September raid provided especially useful oblique photographs of Tarawa.[53] The 2nd Marine Division operations officer, Colonel David M. Shoup, described the photographs as the best of the Pacific War.[54] U.S. planes also took high-quality vertical photographs of Makin.[55]

From this collection of imagery, Joint Intelligence Center Pacific Area of Operations (JICPOA) and division staff prepared intelligence estimates of Japanese troop strength, defenses, and nautical data. In an ingenious use of photographic evidence, 2nd Marine Division staff estimated Tarawa's garrison strength in officers and men from the number and layout of latrines photographed.[56] Intelligence suggested that 2,500–3,100 combat troops were at Tarawa and put Makin's garrison at 500–800 men,

51 Shaw, Nalty, and Turnbladh, *Central Pacific Drive*, 28.

52 Morison, *Aleutians, Gilberts, and Marshalls*, 96 – 99.

53 Ibid., 97, 97n1.

54 Alexander, *Utmost Savagery*, 70.

55 Shaw, Nalty, and Turnbladh, *Central Pacific Drive*, 29.

56 Ibid.

Nautilus (SS-168)

Nautilus was already a war-tested boat by November 1943. Commissioned in 1930, she was at the Mare Island Naval Shipyard for modernization when the Japanese struck Pearl Harbor. She departed Pearl Harbor for her first war patrol on 24 May 1942, bound for Midway to aid in repelling the expected Japanese invasion force. *Nautilus'* first taste of combat was intense. Japanese planes strafed her, enemy ships dropped 42 depth charges on her, and she expended five torpedoes against a Japanese battleship and a carrier. Unfortunately, problems with the Mark XIV torpedo prevented any of her hits from detonating. Continuing her patrol, she operated in waters off Honshu, damaging a Japanese destroyer and an oil tanker and sinking the destroyer *Yamakaze*. Once again, she faced a severe depth charge attack and underwent repairs in July–August 1942.

Nautilus made her first visit to the Gilberts in September 1942, when she transported Marine Lieutenant Colonel Evan Carlson's 2nd Raider Battalion to Makin Atoll. The Marines landed on Butaritari, a future Galvanic objective, on 17–18 August 1942. The raid was ineffective, but alerted the Japanese to their exposed position in the Gilberts, much to the detriment of later United States operations.

Two more patrols followed, including the landing of Army scouts on Attu during the Aleutians campaign on 11 May 1943. The significant role she played in Galvanic only added to the boat's legacy. Her next patrol took her to the waters off Palau, where she sank the 6,070-ton *America Maru* and damaged three other cargo ships.

Beginning in the spring of 1944, most of her patrols took place around the Philippines in support of Allied guerilla forces and reconnaissance operations. *Nautilus* completed her 14th and final war patrol on 30 January 1945, and then proceeded to Philadelphia for inactivation. A legendary boat, *Nautilus* earned the Presidential Unit Citation and 14

estimates that proved to be very accurate.[57] The 2nd Marine Division was also successful in identifying enemy strong points and weapons positions, with the division's enemy situation map of 22 October was proven to have been 90 percent accurate.[58]

What aerial photography could not accurately forecast was oceanographic and tidal information. Vice Admiral Lockwood dispatched *Nautilus* (SS-168) for this purpose. Using the personal camera of her executive officer after Navy-provided equipment failed, she took hundreds of photographs of the islands, identifying a channel into the Tarawa lagoon

57 Crowl and Love, *Seizure of the Gilberts and Marshalls*, 30, 33.

58 Alexander, *Utmost Savagery*, 70.

battle stars for her World War II service. Her successor, SSN-571, the Navy's first nuclear-powered submarine, carried on her storied name and, on 3 August 1958, became the first vessel to reach the geographic North Pole.[1]

***Nautilus* (SS-168) transported Marine Lieutenant Colonel Evan Carlson's 2nd Raider Battalion to Makin Atoll. She earned the Presidential Unit Citation and 14 battle stars for her World War II service (NHHC NH 45666).**

1 "*Nautilus* III (SS-168)," DANFS, https://www.history.navy.mil/research/histories/ship-histories/danfs/n/nautilus-ss-168-iii.html, accessed 13 September 2019.

and estimating hydrographic and beach conditions at each objective. *Nautilus* also provided a panorama of the shorelines, useful for orienting the landing craft coxswains who would deliver the Marines and soldiers to the invasion beaches.[59]

A final, critical gap in American knowledge involved tidal behavior at Betio and Butaritari, coral islands surrounded by a submerged reef. A fully loaded LCVP (landing craft, vehicle, personnel), also known as a Higgins boat, drew about three and a half feet of water. Any less water over the reef would ground these craft hundreds of yards from the beach.

59 Crowl and Love, *Seizure of the Gilberts and Marshalls*, 27; Morison, *Aleutians, Gilberts and Marshalls*, 98; Alexander, *Utmost Savagery*, 70.

To determine tidal conditions, and collect any other relevant intelligence, a 16-man "foreign legion" of officials, sailors, and military officers from Australia, Fiji, and New Zealand assembled in Pearl Harbor. [60] Their collected Gilbert Islands expertise estimated between two and five feet of water over the reef off Betio on D-day. The group, however, warned that Betio was susceptible to "dodging tides," a term for tides with little height variance. Moreover, the operation was scheduled for a neap tide period, when tidal ranges are lowest. Julian Smith judged the chance that LCVPs would clear the reef at 50–50.[61] The ability to traverse Betio's reef therefore became a chief concern for the 2nd Marine Division planners.

REFINING THE PLAN

On 2 October, Julian Smith and his staff arrived at Pearl Harbor to coordinate operational plans for the assault on Betio with Holland Smith and Turner. The Marines presented a plan outlining a bombardment lasting several days, a decoy landing, and the capture of a neighboring island for use as an artillery fire-support base.[62] Fearing that the division's plans threatened to make the force larger, slower, and more visible, Smith and Turner allowed for a preliminary air and sea bombardment of less than three hours and no preliminary or decoy landings.[63] Holland Smith also refused a request to release the division's third regiment, the 6th Marines, from their role as corps reserve, limiting the initial assault on Betio to two regiments. Julian Smith, realizing that his division was going to conduct a frontal assault on a heavily fortified island, requested that Holland Smith issue orders explicitly directing the 2nd Marine Division to carry out this scheme of maneuver, thereby absolving him of responsibility for the plan. Holland Smith granted the division commander's request.[64]

---

60 Dyer, *The Amphibians Came to Conquer*, 718.

61 Alexander, *Utmost Savagery*, 76; Shaw, Nalty, and Turnbladh, *Central Pacific Drive*, 31.

62 Alexander, *Across the Reef*, 4.

63 Shaw, Nalty, and Turnbladh, *Central Pacific Drive*, 36–37.

64 Ibid., 37–38.

Another dispute arising out of the October meeting was 2nd Marine Division's request for landing vehicle, tracked (LVTs), nicknamed "amtrac," for landing operations. Required by agreement to carry out the operation with equipment located in-theater, the Marines hoped to use their amtracs to surmount Betio's reef. The first model of the amphibious vehicle, the LVT-1 Alligator, had been employed by the 2nd Marine Division for carrying supplies ashore at Guadalcanal. Shoup, the division's operations officer, realized the vehicle's potential for delivering troops to shore. The Marines persuaded a New Zealand auto plant to apply boilerplate as improvised armor to the thin-skinned vehicles in anticipation of this use.[65]

After rough use in the South Pacific and during training, however, there were only 75 LVT-1s available. This was too few to carry the three initial assault waves ashore. Julian Smith requested that his Marines be equipped with 100 new and improved LVT-2 Water Buffalos, at the time stockpiled at San Diego. Although Holland Smith agreed, Turner refused, noting that convoys of LSTs (landing ship, tank) would be required to deliver the LVT-2s.[66] A slow-moving LST convoy, approximately 33 percent slower than large transports, would require a separate convoy, additional escorts, and an earlier and direct approach to the objectives. This increased the risk of detection and the loss of surprise.[67] Nimitz had issued an instruction in September to subordinate commanders to use LSTs for amphibious landings only after the assault phase in order to avoid this issue.[68] Holland Smith, however, would not take "no" for an answer. When his heated negotiations with Turner reached an impasse, Smith gave an ultimatum: "No LVTs, no operation."[69] Turner relented, and the Navy ordered 50 LVT-2s to Samoa. Joined there by Marine crews, the LVTs

65 Alexander, *Across the Reef*, 2; Alexander, *Utmost Savagery*, 58–60, 83–84.

66 Alexander, *Across the Reef*, 2.

67 Alexander, *Utmost Savagery*, 60; Dyer, *The Amphibians Came to Conquer*, 655.

68 Ibid.

69 Alexander, *Across the Reef*, 2.

would embark on LSTs and proceed directly to transport areas off Tarawa. The 50 remaining LVT-2s went to Pearl Harbor for Army use at Makin.[70]

THE FINAL OPERATION PLAN

Spruance's 324-page Galvanic operation plan, issued in late October, organized Central Pacific Force into several task forces. Carrier forces, subdivided into four task groups, would make up TF 50. Turner split his assault forces (TF 54) into TF 52, Northern Attack Force, under Turner's direct control with the objective of Makin, and TF 53, Southern Attack Force, under Rear Admiral Harry W. Hill with the objective of Tarawa. Rear Admiral John H. Hoover would command TF 57, including the garrison force and shore-based air.[71]

Although Tarawa would undoubtedly be the most difficult objective, amphibious veterans Turner and Holland Smith chose to station themselves off Makin with TF 52 due to the threat of a Japanese counterattack from Truk. Additionally, the proximity of the Japanese Combined Fleet prompted Spruance to assign roughly equal gunfire-support sections to each target, despite the much larger Japanese numbers on Tarawa. Hill, commanding Southern Attack Force at Tarawa, had previously served on convoy duty in the Atlantic and commanded a battleship division in support of the Guadalcanal campaign. Like most American naval officers in 1943, he had no previous experience with amphibious combat operations.[72]

The air plan called for the carrier force to strike targets in the Marshalls, Gilberts and the nearby phosphate islands in advance of the battle. On D-day and beyond, the plan assigned one task group to each major target, with a third positioned between Makin and the Marshalls to intercept enemy air attacks, and a fourth serving as a reserve and providing air coverage for incoming convoys of garrison troops. Escort

---

70 Shaw, Nalty, and Turnbladh, *Central Pacific Drive*, 39; Alexander, *Utmost Savagery*, 60.

71 Dyer, *The Amphibians Came to Conquer*, 630–32.

72 "Vice Adm. Harry W. Hill Dies; An Ex-Amphibious Commander," *New York Times*, 21 July 1971.

carriers, attached to the invasion task forces, would remain close to the invasion beaches and devote their air squadrons to supporting the landing operations.[73]

In the week preceding the attack, the aircraft of TF 50 and TF 57 would reconnoiter and bomb Tarawa, Makin, and the operational airfields on Nauru and in the Marshalls. A force of cruisers detached from TF 50 would bombard Tarawa on D-1. TF 52 and TF 53 would carry out simultaneous assaults at Betio and Butaritari beginning on the morning of D-day. Three hours of bombardment by sea and air would precede the landings. As the invasion troops took the island, garrison troops and Navy construction battalions, or "Seabees," of TF 57 would be en route to relieve them, with major arrivals scheduled up to D+8.[74] After taking the main islands, the invasion forces would secure the remainder of the atolls. Meanwhile, *Nautilus* would transport a Marine amphibious reconnaissance company to Apamama. It would reconnoiter the island and either seize it or wait for follow-on forces, depending on enemy strength.[75]

On more than one occasion, other officers accused Spruance of using a "sledgehammer," in the guise of a massive concentration of air and sea power, to destroy a relatively small collection of enemy positions.[76] Spruance's reply to one such criticism was characteristically terse: "That's the way to win wars."[77] Central Pacific Force's strength for Galvanic reflected Spruance's belief in the efficacy of overwhelming combat power. The land assault and garrison forces numbered more than 35,000. Fifth Fleet marshalled 12 battleships, 9 heavy cruisers, 5 light cruisers, 6 fleet carriers, 5 light carriers, 8 escort carriers, 58 destroyers, 10 submarines,

---

73 "Annex C to COMTASKFORCE Fifty Four Op Plan A2-43," 23 October 1943, Collection 575, Box 14, Folder A16-3(25), OpPlan A2-43, Annexes C and D, Richmond K. Turner Papers (hereafter Turner Papers), Naval History and Heritage Command, Washington, DC; Morison, *Aleutians, Gilberts and Marshalls*, 336–40.

74 Dyer, *The Amphibians Came to Conquer*, 648.

75 Shaw, Nalty, and Turnbladh, *Central Pacific Drive*, 100.

76 Dyer, *The Amphibians Came to Conquer*, 629.

77 Buell, *The Quiet Warrior*, 170.

and 3 minesweepers. Dozens of transports, cargo ships, and LSTs, and two of the new LSDs (landing ship, dock), *Ashland* (LSD-1) and *Belle Grove* (LSD-2), would support the operation. The LSDs would float M3 Stuart light and M4 Sherman medium tanks, pre-loaded on LCMs (landing craft, mechanized), out of their revolutionary floodable well decks to support the infantry assault. More than 1,100 aircraft of all types would support the invasion.[78] It was the largest American naval force assembled in the Pacific to date.[79]

Amphibious task force en route to Tarawa just before the invasion (NHHC NH 92617).

78 Morison, *Aleutians, Gilberts and Marshalls*, 336–40. These numbers do not include the 198 aircraft of TG 57.4, the Ellice Islands Defense and Utility Group, nor do they account for the precise number of reconnaissance aircraft on battleships and cruisers involved in the operation.

79 Shaw, Nalty, and Turnbladh, *Central Pacific Drive*, 104.

CARRIER RAIDS ON RABAUL

Meanwhile, events in the South Pacific had a major impact on Galvanic's outcome. At a conference of Pacific theater admirals held at Pearl Harbor beginning 25 September, Halsey requested aviation support from the Pacific Fleet for the capture of Bougainville in the northern Solomons, scheduled for 1 November 1943. Spruance insisted on keeping carrier forces concentrated under his command, but the combined arguments of Halsey and Towers convinced Nimitz to dispatch *Saratoga* (CV-3) and *Princeton* (CVL-23) to support the landings.[80] Following service in the South Pacific, the carriers would serve as Task Group (TG) 50.4 for Galvanic. Led by Rear Admiral Frederick C. Sherman, the carriers successfully supported the Bougainville landing.[81]

With the Allies advancing in the South and Southwest Pacific theaters, Imperial Japanese Headquarters stripped the Combined Fleet of 173 carrier aircraft and the entire Second Fleet, along with elements of the Third Fleet, dispatching them to Rabaul.[82] On 5 November, Halsey, aware that Japanese air and sea reinforcements were streaming into Rabaul, ordered Sherman to launch all of his 97 available aircraft at the Japanese bastion.[83] The gambit was a spectacular success, damaging four Japanese heavy cruisers, two light cruisers, and two destroyers while losing only ten aircraft.[84]

80 *Princeton* was built on a *Cleveland*-class cruiser hull, originally commissioned 25 February 1943 as CV-23, and redesignated CVL-23 on 15 July 1943 to identify it as a light carrier. "*Princeton* IV (CV-23)," DANFS, https://www.history.navy.mil/research/histories/ship-histories/danfs/p/princeton-iv.html, accessed 11 July 2019; Reynolds, *Admiral John H. Towers*, 436–38.

81 Samuel Eliot Morison, *History of United States Naval Operations in World War II, Volume Six: Breaking the Bismarcks Barrier, 22 July 1942–1 May 1944* (Boston: Little, Brown and Company, 1954), 292–93.

82 Crowl and Love, *Seizure of the Gilberts and Marshalls*, 69–70.

83 Reynolds, *Admiral John H. Towers*, 445.

84 Morison, *Breaking the Bismarcks Barrier*, 327–28.

The immediate effect was Nimitz's decision to dispatch Spruance's TG 50.3, the Tarawa strike group consisting of *Essex* (CV-9), *Bunker Hill* (CV-17), and *Independence* (CVL-22), to the South Pacific theater, hoping to repeat Sherman's success.[85] The task group would join *Princeton* and *Saratoga* for another raid on Rabaul before returning to Spruance's control. With Spruance's forces scheduled to get underway on 10 November, suddenly it was unclear if any of these five carriers would be available for Galvanic, and it was certain they would not be present for the Marines scheduled dress rehearsal at the island of Efate. Spruance protested, but Nimitz insisted on retaining the timing of the strike, delaying Galvanic one day to 20 November. Montgomery hit Rabaul on 11 November from the north and Sherman from the south, sinking two destroyers. A Japanese aerial counterattack was defeated while suffering heavy losses. In total, the Americans knocked two thirds of the Japanese carrier aircraft sent to Rabaul out of action.[86] The cost to Fifth Fleet was negligible. The light cruiser *Birmingham* (CL-62), damaged by bombs and torpedoes off Bougainville Island on 8 November, was the only ship loaned to Halsey that was scratched from Galvanic.[87]

The November strikes on Rabaul had a profound effect on Galvanic. The Japanese ship and aircraft losses around Bougainville came from among those forces detached from the Combined Fleet. The Japanese at Truk could muster only one carrier without its air group, six battleships, four heavy cruisers, five light cruisers, less than three destroyer squadrons, and 18 submarines against Spruance's armada. Without its carrier aircraft and heavy cruisers, the Combined Fleet was powerless to counter

85 *Independence* was the first in-class of the cruiser-hull light carriers. Commissioned on 14 January 1943 as CV-22, she was redesignated CVL-22 on 15 July 1943. "*Independence* IV (CV-22)," DANFS, https://www.history.navy.mil/research/histories/ship-histories/danfs/i/independence-iv.html, accessed 11 July 2019.

86 Reynolds, *Admiral John H. Towers*, 446; Morison, *Breaking the Bismarcks Barrier*, 330–336; Crowl and Love, *Seizure of the Gilberts and Marshalls*, 69–70.

87 "*Birmingham* II (CL-62)," DANFS, https://www.history.navy.mil/research/histories/ship-histories/danfs/b/birmingham-ii.html, accessed 6 August 2019.

the American invasion of the Gilberts.[88] The most serious threat to the operation was already neutralized as U.S. forces approached the Gilberts. This coup was an early vindication of the proponents of a mutually supporting two-pronged Pacific offensive.

TRAINING

The 2nd Marine Division was a veteran outfit but had grown accustomed to the small-unit-centered combat of jungle warfare. The division required training to prepare for the coordinated large unit tactics necessary for a successful amphibious landing. Training for the landing forces had begun in August with the Marines practicing landings in battalion- and regiment-sized units in and around New Zealand.

Meanwhile, the 27th Infantry Division prepared on Oahu for its first combat operation. The division's officers had conducted a rudimentary amphibious training program for its men prior to its selection for Galvanic. The pace quickened markedly after Marshall assigned the division to the Gilberts operation. Army trainers under General Robert Richardson, Jr., Commanding General, Central Pacific Area, and Holland Smith's VAC split training responsibilities, with the Army conducting ground combat and pre-amphibious training while VAC focused on amphibious and ship-to-shore training.[89]

The attack forces held two full dress rehearsals, with Northern Assault Force practicing on Maui, Territory of Hawaii, and the Southern Attack Force at Efate in the New Hebrides. These exercises, however, lacked realism. The 165th RCT practiced landing with simulated air and gunfire support on Maui between 31 October and 3 November. Unfortunately, when the Northern Task Force provided gunfire support for a live-fire rehearsal, the assault waves did not land for fear of damaging landing craft in rough surf. The same rationale prevented the 165th RCT from practicing land-

---

88 Morison, *Breaking the Bismarcks Barrier*, 336; Morison, *Aleutians, Gilberts and Marshalls*, 137; Alexander, *Utmost Savagery*, 92.

89 Shaw, Nalty, and Turnbladh, *Central Pacific Drive*, 46–47.

ing supplies.[90] The 2nd Marine Division faced similar limitations at Efate between 7 and 13 November. With the carriers attacking Rabaul, there was no practice coordinating between ground and air forces, or between task force leaders. Meanwhile Navy ships practiced gunfire on an entirely different beach, and failed to land LVTs and tanks for fear of attrition.[91]

A final, important phase of training occurred en route to the objectives. The troops learned their destination only upon getting underway from Hawaii and Efate, and Marines, sailors, and soldiers pored over plans, photography, maps, and timetables on board the troopships.[92] Mock-ups of the islands proliferated. Samuel Eliot Morison, embarked on the heavy cruiser *Baltimore* (CA-68) with TF 52, noted that "every ship was a floating college of naval warfare." Turner and Hill exercised their vessels, running anti-aircraft, anti-submarine, gunnery, and tactical drills. The attack groups practiced maximum radio silence to maintain utmost secrecy and Spruance ensured the heavy use of semaphores, lights, and flag-hoist signals.[93] The exertions of Fifth Fleet's crews would pay dividends as they approached their respective objectives.

MOVEMENT TO TARGET AND LOGISTICS

Moving and supplying more than 200 ships and 35,000 men from multiple points across the Pacific to distant objectives required a massive logistical effort. To support this undertaking, the Navy initiated the use of service squadrons (ServRons) in earnest just prior to Galvanic. ServRon 4, the Navy's first floating base, was commissioned on 1 November 1943 and dispatched to Funafuti lagoon with enormous stockpiles of food, medicine, ammunition, and fuel, which were floated by barge to the fleet. To keep the task forces underway to their objective, two fleet oilers accompanied the attack task forces, and a task group of oilers from ServRon 8, escorted by destroyers, ranged throughout the Gilberts during the operation, refu-

90 Crowl and Love, *Seizure of the Gilberts and Marshalls*, 47.

91 Alexander, *Utmost Savagery*, 92–93.

92 Alexander, *Across the Reef*, 7–8.

93 Morison, *Aleutians, Gilberts and Marshalls*, 119.

eling vessels when necessary.[94] Galvanic participant Vice Admiral George C. Dyer described the fleet as an "offensively minded logistical octopus," and Galvanic proved just that.[95]

Warships, transports, and cargo ships weighed anchor in far-flung harbors and roadsteads across the Pacific throughout November. TF 52, Carrier Interceptor Group (TG 50.1), and Northern Carrier Group (TG 50.2) departed Pearl Harbor for Makin on 10 November. The slower LST convoys preceded these forces, the first departing on 31 October with garrison troops and taking a circuitous route, while the second charted a direct, plodding course to Makin with the Army's LVT-2s.[96]

The Marines of the Southern Attack Force, having rendezvoused with Hill's warships at Efate, stood for Tarawa on 13 November. The escort carriers from Espiritu Santo joined the force en route, as did three light cruisers returning from Bougainville on 17 November. The LSTs carrying LVT-2s departed from Samoa and stood directly to the transport zone off Tarawa. The Southern (TG 50.3) and Relief (TG 50.4) Carrier Groups refueled at Espiritu Santo following their strikes on Rabaul, then departed for the Gilberts. The Southern Carrier Group (TG 50.3) sailed roughly parallel to the Southern Attack Force, while the Relief Carrier Group steamed north, directly at its initial objective, the Nauru airfield.[97]

Reconnaissance and intelligence gathering continued up to the eve of D-day. Hoover's TF 57 scoured the islands, conducting reconnaissance, bombing targets, and photographing installations. Planes dropped the final reels of aerial photography, taken while troopships were already underway, by parachute onto the deck of division headquarters on the battleship *Maryland* (BB-46). Quickly interpreted, they provided import-

---

94 Morison, *Aleutians, Gilberts and Marshalls*, 106–108.

95 Dyer, *The Amphibians Came to Conquer*, 597.

96 Morison, *Aleutians, Gilberts and Marshalls*, 114–17; Crowl and Love, *Seizure of the Gilberts and Marshalls*, 57.

97 Morison, *Aleutians, Gilberts and Marshalls*, 117.

ant last-minute tactical intelligence.[98] *Nautilus* also played a key role in last-minute refinement of the invasion plan. Dispatched ahead of the invasion fleet to report weather and tide conditions, the submarine reported that Betio's orientation was off by 11 degrees in the Admiralty charts used to plan the operation. If undetected, this error could have ruined the task force's approach to the island and led to disaster.[99]

En route to their designated areas of operations, the carriers of TF 50 struck targets in the Gilberts and Marshalls. The Carrier Interceptor Group under Pownall delivered 130 tons of ordnance against the Marshalls strongholds of Jaluit and Mili on 19 November. The group then took position north of Makin to intercept any air strikes from the Marshalls.[100] Northern Carrier Group under Rear Admiral Arthur W. Radford hit Butaritari on the same day, dropping 95 tons of bombs. Southern Group under Montgomery launched attacks on Betio on 18 and 19 November, dropping a total of 184 tons of ordnance, and detached three heavy cruisers and two destroyers to bombard the island on the 19th.[101] The bombardment lasted 90 minutes but failed to silence the island's 8-inch coastal defense guns.[102] Relief Carrier Group, the victors of Rabaul, pounded the airfield at Nauru on 19 November. The attack, along with an earlier strike by Hoover's long-range bombers, neutralized the Japanese airfield. Land-based aircraft of TF 57 also bombed Tarawa and Makin in the week preceding the landings.[103]

The Japanese detected the invasion force on 18 November when their patrol aircraft spotted the LSTs approaching Makin. A single bomber attacked the formation at dusk, with another attack the following day. LST

---

98 Thomas J. Cooley, "The Aerial Photo in Amphibious Intelligence," *Marine Corps Gazette* 28 (October 1945): 34.

99 Morison, *Aleutians, Gilberts and Marshalls*, 153–54.

100 Crowl and Love, *Seizure of the Gilberts and Marshalls*, 56.

101 Dyer, *The Amphibians Came to Conquer*, 648.

102 Ibid., 647.

103 Crowl and Love, *Seizure of the Gilberts and Marshalls*, 55; Morison, *Aleutians, Gilberts and Marshalls*, 118; Dyer, *The Amphibians Came to Conquer*, 645.

Turner's Message

On D-1, as the massive fleet approached Makin and Tarawa, all hands received the following message from Admiral Turner as they awaited H-hour.

> Units attached to this force are honored in having been selected to strike another hard blow against the enemy by capturing the Gilbert Islands. The close co-operation between all arms and Services, the spirit of loyalty to each other, and the determination to succeed displayed by veteran and untried personnel alike, gives me complete confidence that we will never stop until we have achieved success. I lift my spirits with this unified team of Army, Navy and Marines whether attached to ships, aircraft, or ground units, and I say to you that I know God will bless you and give you the strength to win a glorious victory.[1]

1 Dyer, *The Amphibians Came to Conquer*, 650.

anti-aircraft gunners and timely intervention from friendly fighter aircraft held off the Japanese planes, splashing two bombers in the process.[104] The LSTs suffered no damage and arrived off Makin on time.

Upon receiving reports of the U.S. fleet's approach, Admiral Koga concluded that an American offensive was underway in the Central Pacific. He ordered eight long-range *I*-class and one *RO*-class submarine toward the Gilberts and Marshalls that same day and redeployed land-based bombers to Truk to reinforce the bare-bones complement of 46 aircraft in the area at the time of the invasion.[105] Hobbled though he was by recent combat losses, Koga would attempt to deliver a blow to the Americans in the Gilberts.

104 Crowl and Love, *Seizure of the Gilberts and Marshalls*, 58–59.

105 "Chuby Taiheiyo Rikugen Sakusen (Army Operations in the Central Pacific Vol.1) Senshi Sosho #6," translated by Bunichi Ohtsuka, Collection 5239, Box 30, 6, Joseph H. Alexander Papers (hereafter Alexander Papers), United States Marine Corps Archives, Quantico, VA; Clay Blair Jr., *Silent Victory: The U.S. Submarine War Against Japan* (New York: J. B. Lippincott Company, 1975), 508; Alexander, *Utmost Savagery*, 109; Morison, *Aleutians, Gilberts and Marshalls*, 138.

BOMBARDMENT AND ASSAULT PLANS

The assault phase of Galvanic relied upon similar plans for naval air and gunfire support at Betio and Butaritari. The landings at Betio would feature a 30-minute carrier strike on the islands starting at 0545 on 20 November. From the termination of the air strikes, termed W-hour, until 0805, warships would bombard the island. Firing would cease for five minutes only to open again at 0810, focusing on the beaches and catching any defenders who prematurely exited bomb shelters to meet the assault. Naval gunfire would then continue up to 0825. At this point carrier aircraft would again attack enemy positions at and beyond the beaches for five minutes just before the first waves landed at 0830, designated H-hour. Following the landing, aircraft would attack defenses farther inland. After the ground forces were ashore, aircraft and gunfire-support ships would stand by to engage targets of opportunity and respond to requests for support from ground forces. [106] Rear Admiral Howard Kingman, Fire Support Group commander, summarized his plan during a briefing: "It is not our intention to wreck the island. We do not intend to destroy it. Gentlemen, we will obliterate it."[107]

The 2nd Marine Division would land in a three-battalion front on the north, lagoon side of the island, with two battalion landing teams of the 2nd Marine Regiment, Landing Team (LT) 2/2 and LT 3/2, and one from the 8th Marines, LT 2/8. In addition to their organic composition, each battalion had attached a shore fire-control party, combat engineers from the 18th Marine Regiment, and other support and logistical elements to form a landing team. The 2nd Tank Battalion and Company C, I Marine

---

106 "Annex C to CTF 53 OPORD A104-43 (revised): Gunfire Support Plan," Collection 140, Box 2, Folder: Plans A103-343-A105-43, 1–8, Harry W. Hill Papers (hereafter Hill Papers), Naval History and Heritage Command, Washington, D.C; "Appendix 4 to Annex C to CTF 53 OPORD A104-43 (Revised): Gunfire and Air Support Time Schedule," 4 November 1943, Collection 140, Box 2, Folder: A103-43-A105-43, 1–2, Hill Papers; Dyer, *The Amphibians Came to Conquer*, 690–91.

107 Quoted in Ian W. Toll, *The Conquering Tide: War in the Pacific Islands, 1942–1944* (New York: W. W. Norton & Company, 2015), 365.

Amphibious Corps (IMAC) Tank Battalion would provide armor support. A battalion of 75-mm pack howitzers from the 10th Marine Regiment (1/10) was also tasked to land on Betio on D-day. One battalion of the 2nd Marines, LT 1/2, was held in regimental reserve, and two battalions of the 8th Marines, LTs 1/8 and 3/8, were designated the division reserve.[108]

Maryland (BB-46) fires her forward 16-inch/45-caliber guns at Tarawa (NHHC 80-G-54397).

108 Alexander, *Across the Reef*, 5–6; Shaw, Nalty, and Turnbladh, *Central Pacific Drive*, 64–65; Alexander, *Utmost Savagery*, 56, 141–42.

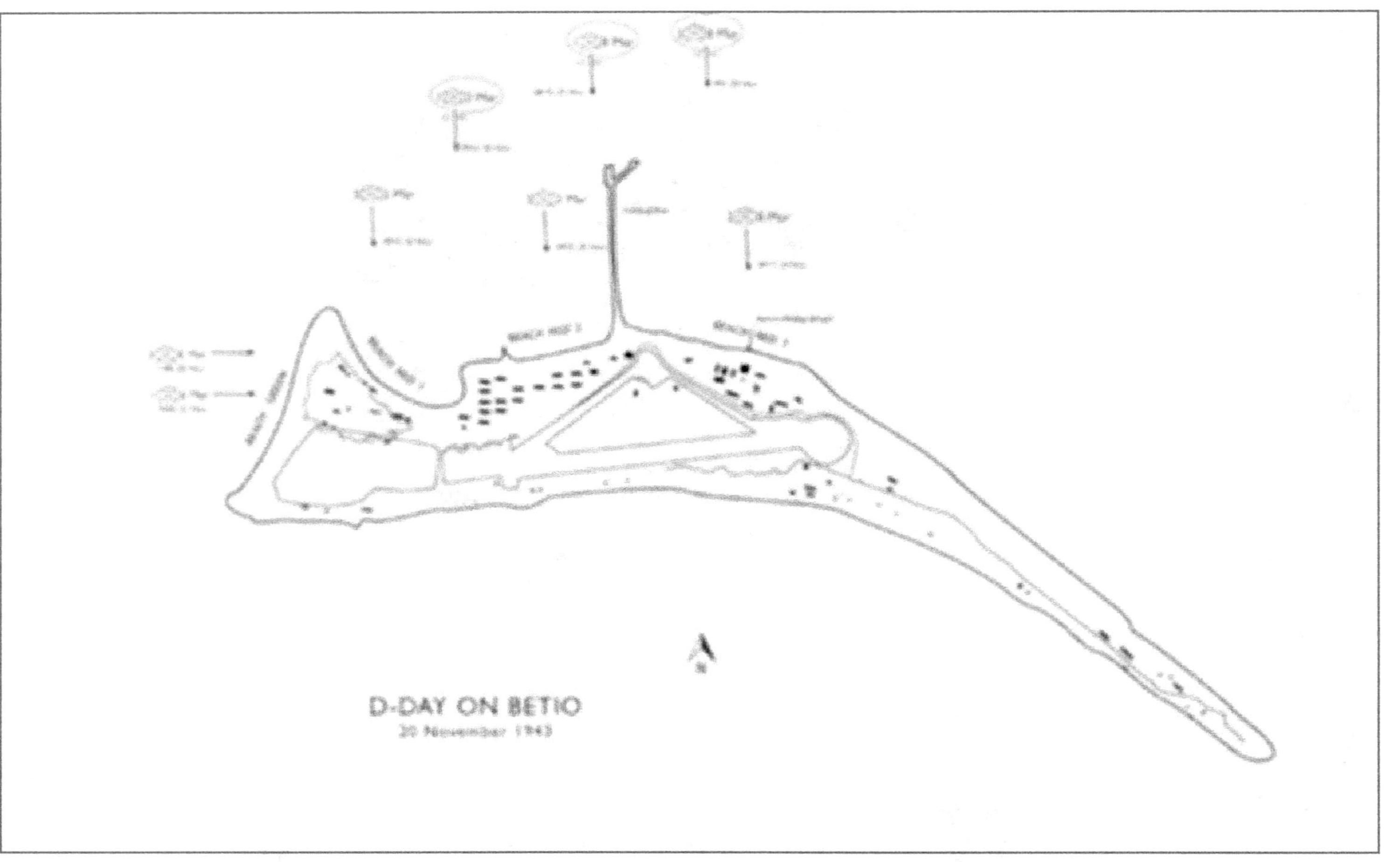
D-DAY ON BETIO
20 November 1943

Planners selected a northern landing for several reasons. First, VAC and 2nd Marine Division planners knew from aerial photography that the Japanese had heavily fortified and mined the seaward approaches to the island, and they expected strong and variable currents on those approaches. Information on the lagoon side of the island was less certain, but U.S. planners knew that the defensive positions on the lagoon were weaker and reasoned that the Japanese would leave an open route to the wharves to enable movement and resupply by ship. The lagoon would also provide an easier water route for ships and boats to maneuver toward the beaches. Once the Marines were ashore, landing perpendicular to the island's long axis avoided the necessity of fighting through enemy defenses in depth, from one end of the island to another, and the broad front formed by the landings would maximize the area available to land supplies and maneuver. Finally, the north shoreline of Betio had definite landmarks separating the landing beaches. Red 1, on the western flank, was in a concave bay, and a long pier that reached the seaward edge of the reef separated Red 2 and Red 3, the easternmost beach.[109]

Cooperation with Navy forces was essential for a successful landing operation. A minesweeper would clear the entrance to the lagoon, and another would enter with two destroyers. As the destroyers provided direct fire support, the first minesweeper would mark the line of departure for the LVTs of the first three assault waves. Next, LCVPs and LCMs would attempt to float over the reef with the rest of the Marines, as well as tanks, artillery, and supplies. If these grounded, however, LVTs could shuttle back and forth to the reef, evacuating wounded to the waiting LCVPs and bringing fresh Marines to the beach.[110]

At Makin, the 27th Infantry Division would land in two areas on the hammer-shaped island, with Red beaches lying on the island's western hammerhead and Yellow beaches situated on the northern, lagoon side of the island's long axis, between one and a half and three miles northeast of the Red beaches. As at Betio, a 30-minute aerial bombardment

109 Shaw, Nalty, and Turnbladh, *Central Pacific Drive*, 31.

110 Dyer, *The Amphibians Came to Conquer*, 696–97.

would precede the landings, followed by naval gunfire for one hour and 45 minutes, followed by a five-minute air strike against the beaches. Naval gunfire would then shift inland, beyond the invasion beaches. H-hour at Red 1 and Red 2 was 0830. Hoping to catch the Japanese forces in a pincer movement if they concentrated against the Red beaches, H-Hour at Yellow 1, Yellow 2, and Yellow 3 was at 1030. A minesweeper would clear the way and two destroyers would provide close-range fire support for the Yellow beach landings. LVTs would carry the first wave of troops to each set of beaches, with follow-on waves in LCVPs and LCMs carrying light and medium tanks.[111]

PRE-LANDING BOMBARDMENT: BETIO

Southern Attack Force approached Tarawa in the pre-dawn hours of 20 November, sailing eastward parallel to and south of Betio before winding clockwise around the island, terminating at the designated transport area eight miles to its northwest. Along this procession, fire-support sections slipped away from the main force, coiling around the target to the south, southwest and northwest.[112] In these designated fire-support areas, three old battleships, four cruisers, and nine destroyers of the Gunfire Support Group awaited W-hour in the darkness.

The Japanese' first acknowledgment of the Americans' presence was a red star-cluster flare lofted from the island approximately at 0441. The 8-inch Japanese coastal guns opened the Battle of Tarawa at long range at 0507.[113] *Maryland* answered as warships and other coastal guns joined the brawl. At general quarters on board *Tennessee* (BB-43), a Marine watched *Santa Fe* (CL-60) engage a Japanese battery. "There would be a whirling sheet of orange flame from the cruisers' guns," he recalled, "and then a couple of red balls would streak through the blackness toward the

111 Crowl and Love, *Seizure of the Gilberts and Marshalls*, 75–77, 82–83.

112 "Approach Plan, Appendix 1 to Annex X to OpOrder A 103-43," 4 November 1943, Collection 140, Box 2, Folder: A103-43-A105-43, Hill Papers.

113 Morison, *Aleutians, Gilberts and Marshalls*, 156; Dyer, *The Amphibians Came to Conquer*, 692.

island. Then the enemy shore battery would answer by another yellow flash hurling a meteor across the sea at the cruiser."[114] "Old Mary's" fifth salvo touched off a tremendous explosion on the island and the battery temporarily went silent.[115]

Unfortunately, *Maryland*, jury-rigged as Hill's command vessel, carried her communication central on a wing of her flag bridge, at roughly the same level as the muzzles of her 16-inch guns.[116] In addition to a recurring problem with mutual interference from the many radios wedged into close proximity on the ship, *Maryland's* first salvo knocked out certain channels of communication with headquarters. This was the first incident in a constant theme of poor radio communications during Galvanic.[117]

The Fire Support Group checked its fire at approximately 0542 in preparation for the arrival of aircraft from Task Group 50.3.[118] The air strike scheduled for 0545, however, did not materialize. As the island guns continued to fire, focusing largely on the transport area, the Americans eyed their watches and the sky. Hill, embarked onboard *Maryland*, was unable to contact his carriers due to the radio malfunction. With his patience exhausted, Hill used short-range talk between ships (TBS) to order his warships to resume fire in order to protect the transports from Japanese shore batteries at approximately 0600. As the counter-battery fire resumed, he ordered the transports northward, away from the island. The American guns fired for only a few minutes before the aircraft arrived, commencing attacks at 0613.[119]

The reason for the delay in the air strike is unclear. One culprit may have been changes to Carrier Task Force orders born out of the Northern

114 Roger M. Emmons, "Tarawa Bombardment," *Marine Corps Gazette* (March 1948): 43–44.

115 Dyer, *The Amphibians Came to Conquer*, 693; Alexander, *Across the Reef*, 14.

116 Dyer, *The Amphibians Came to Conquer*, 611, 692–93.

117 Shaw, Nalty, and Turnbladh, *Central Pacific Drive*, 107–108; Alexander, *Utmost Savagery*, 101.

118 Alexander, *Utmost Savagery*, 101; Dyer, *The Amphibians Came to Conquer*, 693.

119 Dyer, *The Amphibians Came to Conquer*, 690, 693–94; Alexander, *Utmost Savagery*, 102.

Attack Force dress rehearsal in Maui, changing the timing of the strike to coincide with sunrise. Turner approved the alteration, but Hill never received notice of the change. A complete breakdown in communication between Turner, Hill, Montgomery, and Pownall resulted in conflicting understandings of the strike's timetable. In addition, the aircraft had difficulty forming up in the pre-dawn light, delaying the attack further.[120] The aircraft continued the bombardment for seven minutes instead of the planned 30. Hill declared W-hour at 0620.[121]

The following bombardment shook the island for over two hours. The warships approached the island by type, battlewagons leading the procession, followed by cruisers, then destroyers, some steaming within 2,000 yards of the island. As H-hour approached warships lay-to northwest of the island and provided the planned enfilading fire. With the exception of some pre-selected targets, the gunfire-support plan intended to saturate designated areas, and the island as a whole. In all, the warships lobbed an estimated 3,000 tons of projectiles at Betio during the preparatory bombardment.[122]

Undoubtedly, the destroyers of Fire Support Section 4 drew the most dangerous assignment in the Fire Support Group. Shortly after W-hour, *Ringgold* (DD-500) and *Dashiell* (DD-659) left picket duty and steamed to the mouth of the lagoon. With LCVPs from troopship *Monrovia* (AP-64) laying obscuration from smoke pots, minesweepers *Pursuit* (AM-108) and *Requisite* (AM-109) cleared a channel through the barrier reef, finding no mines. Spotter aircraft helped *Pursuit* mark submerged reefs and obstacles. The destroyers entered the swept channel with 5-inch guns blazing at 0708, *Ringgold* at the lead with pilot and "Foreign Legion" officer Lieutenant Gordon Webster, Royal New Zealand Naval Reserve, at the con. Tasked with engaging the Japanese from inside the lagoon, Commander Henry Crommelin had informed his men that *Ringgold* was

120 Dyer, *The Amphibians Came to Conquer*, 709–11.

121 Richmond K. Turner, "Commander Task Force 53 Report of Tarawa Operations," 13 December 1943, Box 7, Folder A16-39, CTF 53, Enclosure A, 9, Turner Papers.

122 Morison, *Aleutians, Gilberts and Marshalls*, 157.

to be the "honor" ship for the invasion of Tarawa.[123] Proceeding at five knots and unable to maneuver in the channel with Japanese guns 7,000 yards away on her starboard bow, *Ringgold* was a sitting duck.[124]

Just as she broke into the lagoon, Japanese shells struck *Ringgold* twice. Both 5-inch shells proved to be duds, the first deflecting off the barrel of the No. 5 torpedo mount and crashing into the sick bay, effectively destroying it. The second burst into the after engine room at the waterline and lodged in a switchboard.[125] Water rushed in from a two-foot-by-nine-inch hole. Lieutenant Wayne Parker, engineering officer, sat on the gash and stopped the flooding with his body. He supervised the patching of the hole, and then he reportedly ordered the space cleared and, with assistance from several men, carried the live shell topside and threw it into the lagoon. Parker later received the Navy Cross.[126] *Ringgold* continued to fight, firing 325 5-inch shells in the first hour of action. *Dashiell* added another 264 rounds of counter-battery fire and both "tin cans" raked the beach with machine-gun fire as H-hour approached.[127]

Hill altered the bombardment plan at 0749. He believed carrier aircraft from TG 50.3 would not be able to return in time to strafe the landing beaches before H-hour. He instead assigned the task to the pilots of escort carriers *Nassau* (CVE-16) and *Barnes* (CVE-20) at 0749, less than 40 minutes before scheduled landings. In the rush to get the aircraft aloft, the

---

123 Jenny Souviner Hallett, *Preservation of Honor: The U.S.S. Ringgold DD500 Legacy* (s.p., 1998), 67.

124 "USS RINGGOLD—Act Rep, OP 'GALVANIC'," 1 December 1943, 10, 17–18, Record Group 38: Records of the Office of the Chief of Naval Operations, 1875–2006, Series: World War II War Diaries, Other Operational Records and Histories, ca. 1/1/1942–ca. 6/1/1946 (hereafter World War II War Diaries).

125 Ibid.

126 S.A. McCornock, "Conduct of Subordinates During Action, 19, 20, and 21 November, 1943," December 1, 1943, Collection 575, Box 9, Folder A16-3, USS *Ringgold*, Nov.–Dec. 1943, 1–2, Turner Papers; "Wayne Arthur Parker," *Oklahoma History Center*, https://www.okhistory.org/historycenter/militaryhof/inductee.php?id=306, accessed 9 August 2019.

127 Alexander, *Utmost Savagery*, 100.

pilots did not receive an important facet of the instructions. Plans called for aircraft to time the strafing runs based on the location of the landing craft and their distance from the beach, not the pre-scheduled H-hour.[128] The landing craft were late and Hill delayed H-hour to 0900. Nevertheless, the jeep carrier pilots strafed the beaches at 0825 with the craft far off.[129]

The air strikes continued until 0854, when Hill ordered a cease-fire. The assault waves, however, were still 20 minutes away. The carrier aircraft performed a truncated second strafing with low ammunition at 0855, and still too far in advance of the LVTs.[130] When the aircraft moved off the beach Hill did not allow warships to resume fire. Smoke and dust raised from the bombardment obscured the scene in the lagoon, and Hill worried that his guns would hit the incoming landing craft. This decision clearly irked the destroyers in the lagoon, who could see the delayed position of the landing craft clearly. The gunnery officer on *Dashiell* wrote after the battle:

> In this case everything was very clear and the necessity for continuing fire appeared to be quite obvious but it could not be continued because of a schedule and because apparently the Commanding Officers of Fire Support [section] #4 [in the *Dashiell*] could not be depended upon to make a clear estimate of the situation when they were only 1500 yards from the scene of action and the controlling authority was over the horizon.[131]

As a result, there was no significant fire on Betio from 0854 until after the first Marines landed. For more than 15 minutes, the Japanese

---

128 Dyer, *The Amphibians Came to Conquer*, 690, 711–12; Alexander, *Utmost Savagery*, 105.

129 Morison, *Aleutians, Gilberts and Marshalls*, 159–160; Alexander, *Utmost Savagery*, 105; Rear Adm. H.W. Hill, "Tarawa Operations—report of," 13 December1943, Collection 575, Box 7, Folder A16-3, CTF 53, Nov. 1943, 10, Turner Papers.

130 Dyer, *The Amphibians Came to Conquer*, 691.

131 *Dashiell* Action Report, December 5, 1943, quoted in Dyer, *The Amphibians Came to Conquer*, 708.

recovered, moved across the island to battle stations, and prepared for the attack.[132]

BETIO LANDINGS

The first three assault waves crossed the line of departure for the beaches beginning at 0824.[133] The older LVT-1s made less than 4 knots instead of the expected 4 ½ knots used to plan the landing timeline. This slower than anticipated pace only added to the desynchronization of the fire support plan.[134] As the amtracs covered the final 6,000-plus yards to the beach, they came under fire from Japanese defenses that remained quite functional despite the heavy bombardment. Rear Admiral Shibasaki's anti-boat guns, 13-mm heavy machine guns, and mortars proved to be zeroed and able to deliver accurate and deadly fire into the lagoon.[135] The decisive moment came as the LVTs struck the reef, shuddered as their tracks bit into the coral, then crawled over and continued toward the beaches. A Japanese warrant officer watching from his fighting position recalled that upon seeing the LVTs cross the reef, one of his men exclaimed, "The god of death has come!"[136]

The first three waves advanced without undue difficulty in spite of the Japanese fire. The first Marines into action were the 2nd Marine Division scout-snipers under First Lieutenant William D. Hawkins, who seized the end of the long pier at 0855 and began clearing it of Japanese troops.[137] The first Marine LVT touched down on Red 1 at 0910, followed by those on Red 3 at 0917 and Red 2 at 0922. Fifteen hundred Marines had landed

---

132 Alexander, *Utmost Savagery*, 109.

133 Ibid., 105.

134 Shaw, Nalty, and Turnbladh, *Central Pacific Drive*, 56; Dyer, *The Amphibians Came to Conquer*, 697, 699, 700–701.

135 Alexander, *Utmost Savagery*, 108, 111–13.

136 Ibid., 111.

137 Shaw, Nalty, and Turnbladh, *Central Pacific Drive*, 57.

on Betio's beaches in a span of fifteen minutes, losing only 8 of 87 LVTs to Japanese fire in the process.[138]

Despite this accomplishment, the situation on the beaches quickly devolved into chaos as the Marines suffered heavy casualties from well-prepared Japanese positions situated only yards from the sea wall. For all of the ordnance delivered against the tiny island, the pre-landing bombardment had been a manifest failure. The initial assault waves bogged down under heavy enemy fire, unable to advance more than a few yards beyond the cover provided by the sea wall and the pier between Red 2 and 3. The situation was worst at Red 1 and Red 2, while LT 2/8 on Red 3 suffered relatively few casualties.[139]

Led by Major Henry P. Crowe, the Marines on Red 3 maintained the best communications of all the landing teams. With Shore Fire Control Party No. 82 at his disposal, Crowe established communications with *Ringgold* and *Dashiell* at 1030, enabling effective gunfire support on Red 3's eastern flank. *Dashiell* commenced fire immediately and *Ringgold* relieved her at 1043, firing 100 rounds in the next 20 minutes. The destroyers maneuvered dangerously close to the reef, placing 5-inch rounds within 25 meters of the Marines' front lines. This support to LT 2/8 was critical in preventing heavier casualties on Red 3.[140]

The volume and accuracy of Japanese fire only increased as subsequent waves attempted to land in LCVPs. As had been feared, the Higgins boats could not clear the reef, and many Marines waded the several hundred yards toward shore while under fire. LVTs from the first three waves began to ferry wounded back to the reef to exchange for Marines heading to the beaches, but the unnerving accuracy of the Japanese firing began to stall the assault's momentum. Anti-boat guns and 13-mm machine guns sank many LVTs and boats and inflicted high casualties. Enemy fire killed Lieutenant Colonel Herbert R. Amey, Jr., commanding LT 2/2 at Red 2, in the fourth wave. Lieutenant Colonel Walter Jordan, an observer from the

138 Alexander, *Utmost Savagery*, 113, 116.

139 Ibid., 117–20.

140 Ibid., 136.

4th Marine Division, assumed command at Red 2. Following the first three battalions, Julian Smith committed LT 1/2, the 2nd Marines' regimental reserve, to Red 2 and LT 3/8, one half the division reserve, to Red 3. Both landing teams suffered heavy casualties approaching the beaches.[141] The tanks meant to support the assault also fared poorly. By day's end, only 2 of 14 Sherman tanks were still operational, many foundering in shell holes between the reef and the beaches, and others knocked out by Japanese fire. Japanese guns sank all four of the LCMs carrying light tanks before they reached the reef.[142]

Marines wade through the surf off Tarawa. Landing craft brought them to within 500 yards of the beach, but the coral bottom prevented the craft coming any closer to the shore (NHHC UA 55.01.06).

141 Ibid., 133–35.

142 Ibid., 126–28.

Colonel David M. Shoup

Colonel David M. Shoup's personal courage and cool thinking under fire proved crucial to the 2nd Marine Division's success at Betio. An Indiana native, Shoup had been a Marine officer since 1926, and had served in China and various stateside positions in the interwar period. Shoup was serving with the 6th Marines in Iceland at the time of the United States' entry into World War II in December 1941. Returning to San Diego, he joined the 2nd Marine Division in the summer of 1942 as the assistant division operations and training officer. Promoted to lieutenant colonel in September 1942, he served as the G-3 (division operations and training officer) until November 1943. He suffered a minor wound while acting as an observer with the Army's 43rd Infantry Division at Rendova, New Georgia, in the summer of 1943.[1]

Colonel William M. Marshall commanded the 2nd Marine Regiment, one of three regiments in the 2nd Marine Division, on the eve of Galvanic. In a fateful decision, Julian Smith relieved Marshall during pre-invasion training at Efate, allegedly due to health issues, and promoted Shoup to Colonel and command of the regiment. With his unit embarked on several troop transports, Shoup moved from ship to ship, familiarizing himself with the officers and men of his command. His regiment would provide the bulk of the first several assault waves at Betio.[2]

During the fighting on Betio, Shoup proved to be a steadfast example of leadership for his embattled Marines. He would receive the Medal of Honor for his actions. His citation summarized his contributions to victory at Betio:

> Although severely shocked by an exploding shell soon after landing at the pier, and suffering from a serious painful leg wound which had become infected, Colonel Shoup fearlessly exposed himself to the terrific relentless artillery, and rallying his hesitant troops by his own inspiring heroism, gallantly led them across the fringing reefs to charge the heavily fortified island and reinforced our hard-pressed thinly-held lines. Upon arrival at the shore, he assumed command of all landed troops and, working without rest under constant withering enemy fire during the next two days, conducted smashing attacks against unbelievably strong and fanatically defended Japanese positions, despite innumerable obstacles and heavy casualties. By his brilliant leadership, daring tactics, and selfless devotion to duty, Colonel Shoup was largely responsible for the final,

1 "General David M. Shoup," https://www.usmcu.edu/Research/Marine-Corps-History-Division/Information-for-Units/Medal-of-Honor-Recipients-By-Unit/Col-David-Monroe-Shoup/, accessed 13 September 2019.

2 Alexander, *Utmost Savagery*, 93–94.

decisive defeat of the enemy and his indomitable fighting spirit reflects great credit upon the United States Naval Service.3

Shoup was appointed chief of staff for the 2nd Marine Division in December 1943, and served in that capacity through the battles for Saipan and Tinian. He returned to the United States in October 1944 to serve at Headquarters Marine Corps. A variety of post-war assignments included division chief of staff for 1st Marine Division, commanding officer of the Basic School, and inspector general for recruit training following the drowning of six Marine recruits at Parris Island, South Carolina, in 1956. Shoup then served as inspector general for the Marine Corps, and commanded the 1st and 3rd Marine Divisions prior to his selection in 1959 by President Dwight D. Eisenhower to serve as the 22nd Commandant of the Marine Corps.[4] General Shoup retired in 1963 and became an outspoken opponent of the Vietnam War in his post–Marine Corps years.[5]

Colonel David M. Shoup commanded the 2nd Marine Regiment during the fighting on Betio. He received the Medal of Honor for extraordinary heroism (National Archives 74240994).

3 "USS *Shoup*," https://www.public.navy.mil/surfor/ddg86/Pages/Namesake.aspx, accessed September 13, 2019.

4 "General David M. Shoup."

5 "Gen. David M. Shoup Dead at 78; Ex-Commandant of Marine Corps," https://www.nytimes.com/1983/01/16/obituaries/gen-david-m-shoup-dead-at-78-ex-commandant-of-marine-corps.html, accessed 13 September 2019.

Fierce Japanese resistance and chronic problems with U.S. radios meant that for the first 24 hours of combat both sides were in a slugging match with little higher coordination. Colonel Shoup, promoted to command of the 2nd Marine Regiment on the eve of the invasion and tasked with command of all forces ashore during the initial assault, spent several hours struggling ashore under fire from the end of the long pier to the beach. Gaining the beach at 1200, he worked tirelessly to gain situational awareness and exercise command and control from the blind side of a Japanese bunker still occupied by its defenders. Though Shoup was one of a few leaders with an operational radio and could generally communicate with Hill and Smith onboard *Maryland*, he was often frustrated due to the poor radio communications with subordinate units.[143] The reports from Betio were enough to induce Julian Smith to request release of the corps reserve, the 6th Marine Regiment. Hill concurred and relayed Smith's request to Turner, noting, "Issue in doubt." Turner gave Smith control of the 6th Marines two hours later.[144]

In ferocious fighting employing flamethrowers, grenades, and small arms at close range, the Marines managed to carve out a shallow beachhead at Red 3 and part of Red 2 nearest to the pier. Elements of Major Mike Ryan's Company L, in LT 3/2's fourth wave at Red 1, made an inadvertent, but fortuitous, landing on Betio's western hammerhead, designated Green beach, when Japanese fire caused the wading Marines to veer around the point of the so-called "beak" separating the northern from western beaches. Ryan found Green beach to be a much more feasible approach and he began to establish a beachhead with the stragglers of subsequent waves that had also sought shelter from the concentrated Japanese fire on Red 1.[145] In another fortunate development, as daylight faded, the few remaining operational LVTs brought most of the 75-mm pack howitzers of 1/10 Marines to the left flank of Red Two, with the rest manhandled ashore through the surf under fire. The Marines would have

143 Ibid., 133–35, 137; Alexander, *Across the Reef*, 16.

144 Alexander, *Utmost Fury*, 140–41.

145 Ibid., 120–21.

direct-fire artillery support in the morning.[146] By the end of the first day, around 5,000 Marines had landed on Betio, 1,500 of whom were casualties.[147]

Marine throwing a grenade during the fight for Betio Island, circa 20–23 November 1943 (NHHC USMC 63658).

In addition to protecting LT 2/8's left flank, the destroyers seem to have achieved a key success that went unrecognized until much later. At some point during the afternoon of D-day, Rear Admiral Shibasaki decided to relocate from a massive blockhouse located east of Red 3. When he emerged from the blockhouse with his staff, a U.S. shell killed the admiral and his entire staff, rendering the Japanese defenders leaderless within

146 Ibid., 176.

147 Ibid., 150.

Navy Medicine at Tarawa

At Betio, Navy doctors and corpsmen dealt with overwhelming numbers of casualties while under fire ashore with the Marines and on multiple ships that lacked dedicated medical facilities equal to the task. In one case, a Navy doctor and three corpsmen treated 126 patients during the first 36 hours of the operation in a captured Japanese bunker, losing only four patients while fending off attacks from supposedly dead Japanese soldiers more than once.[1] Navy ships of all types became aid stations as Marine casualties were ferried back from the beaches. Despite the destruction of her sick bay by enemy fire, *Ringgold* treated 47 wounded Marines while on station in the lagoon.[2] Even the two small minesweepers treated 60 wounded Marines while marking the line of departure.[3] Faced with a flood of casualties, Rear Admiral Hill took the risk of ordering attack transport *Doyen* (APA-1) into the lagoon early on D+1. The ship's six-man surgical team treated more than 550 severely wounded Marines over the next three days.[4] Two Navy doctors and 28 corpsmen paid the ultimate price at Betio, with an additional two doctors and 57 corpsmen wounded.[5]

1 Alexander, *Utmost Savagery*, 140.
2 Hallett, *Preservation of Honor*, 70.
3 Alexander, *Utmost Savagery*, 270n37.
4 Alexander, *Across the Reef*, 32.
5 Shaw, Nalty, and Turnbladh, *Central Pacific Drive*, 636.

a few hours of the American landings.[148] As night fell, American forces anxiously anticipated a Japanese counterattack. With Shibasaki dead and Japanese communications hampered by bombardment, the counterattack never came.[149]

Meanwhile, the Marines of the division reserve, LT 1/8, spent a miserable night embarked in their LCVPs beyond the reef. The following morning at 0615, LT 1/8 attempted to land on Red 2. Shoup had radioed back and specified that any landing must take place close to the pier, but the approaching LCVPs veered too far west, directly into the teeth of the Japanese defenses. As in previous waves, their boats could not clear the reef and the men of LT 1/8 began to wade from the reef to the beach while under intense fire. The Marines already ashore watched helplessly as 1/8

148 Ibid., 147–49.

149 Ibid., 150–52.

A wounded man receives blood plasma at an aid station on a Betio Island beach, 22 November 1943 (NHHC USMC 67703).

struggled toward the beach, bearing the full brunt of the Japanese fire and sustaining approximately 50 percent casualties.[150]

Despite the slaughter of 1/8, the tide began to shift later that morning. In the words of historian Joseph Alexander, "The ultimate American victory at Betio evolved from the attack executed during one intense hour the second morning by the hodgepodge assortment of Marines and sailors fighting under the leadership of Major Ryan on Green beach."[151] Ryan had spent much of the previous night preparing a combined arms assault on the western end of the island, integrating two Sherman tanks, tactical aircraft, and naval gunfire in support of his attacking Marines. Critically, Navy Lieutenant Thomas Greene, a gunfire spotter with a functioning radio, joined Ryan overnight.[152] *Santa Fe* and *Frazier* (DD-607) provided

150 Ibid., 160–164.

151 Ibid., 159.

152 Ibid., 169.

gunfire support against Japanese strong points before the assault began.[153] Ryan's men attacked from north to south beginning at 1120, seizing all of Green beach by 1225.[154]

As reports of Ryan's success filtered back to Shoup and Julian Smith, Smith planned to employ the 6th Marines, the corps reserve. Now presented with an opportunity to put an intact landing team ashore, Smith ordered LT 1/6 to land via rubber boats at Green beach. He also dispatched LT 2/6 to Bairiki Island, southeast of Betio, to "seal the back door" and establish an artillery firing position—ironically a feature of 2nd Marine Division's original concept for the Betio operation. Smith placed LT 3/6 on standby to land at any assigned spot.[155] These operations took much longer than anticipated, hampered by bad radio communications, poor load plans aboard several ships, and ships getting underway due to reported submarine contacts. LTs 1/6 and 2/6 had finally landed by dusk, the first battalions to make it ashore virtually unscathed.[156] The Marines now had eight infantry and two artillery battalions landed on Betio and Bairiki, with one more infantry battalion available to commit to the fight.[157]

Meanwhile, Shoup could sense the tide turning. Reports began to reach him of *rikusentai* filtering off the island or committing suicide in their positions. At approximately 1600, Shoup transmitted a message to Julian Smith that later became famous: "Casualties: many. Percentage dead: unknown. Combat efficiency: We are winning."[158] That evening, Colonel Merritt "Red Mike" Edson, Julian Smith's chief of staff, made it ashore and assumed overall command.[159] Although the Japanese still mar-

---

153 "USS SANTA FE—Act Rep, Assault on TARAWA, 11/19-25/43," 7–8, 37, World War II War Diaries; "USS FRAZIER—War Diary, 11/1-30/43," 327, World War II War Diaries.

154 Alexander, *Utmost Savagery*, 168–70.

155 Ibid., 172.

156 Ibid., 176.

157 Ibid., 178.

158 Ibid., 174.

159 Ibid., 178.

shalled large numbers of combat troops on the island, no counterattack came on the second night.[160]

Marines on Betio fire from behind a sandbag parapet (National Archives 32606711).

At 0400 on 22 November, Edson issued attack orders. The Marines at Green beach would attack east toward the airfield and Red beaches, while those on Red 2 would attack west, clearing Japanese defenses between Red 1 and Red 2, and those on Red 3 would attack the Japanese strong point on their eastern flank.[161] Fighting remained fierce, but the Marines broke out of their beachheads at Red 2 and Green beaches, and began to eliminate pockets of Japanese resistance throughout the morning.[162] A Japanese bunker complex east of Red 3 stymied American efforts for most of the

160 Ibid., 178–79.

161 Ibid., 180.

162 Ibid., 182–86.

day until First Lieutenant Alexander "Sandy" Bonnyman led an attack that finally eliminated the last Japanese resistance there. Having spent much of the previous day studying the strong point while pinned down, Bonnyman led the clearance of the final bunker in the position with a section of combat engineers. Bonnyman died in the final stages of the attack, an action captured on film by a Marine combat cameraman. For his heroism, he would posthumously receive the Medal of Honor.[163]

First Lieutenant Alexander Bonnyman, Jr., USMCR, posthumously received the Medal of Honor for conspicuous gallantry and intrepidity (National Archives 74240869).

Julian Smith arrived at Edson and Shoup's command post around 1400, having learned first-hand the realities of Japanese resistance as his landing craft took fire, killing the coxswain and disabling the boat.[164] Smith assumed command of operations ashore at 1930 and prepared orders for the next day's operation. His final uncommitted battalion, LT 3/6, would land at Green beach, pass through LT 1/6, and continue the attack to the east, while the 2nd Marines under Shoup would continue reducing Japanese positions west of Red 1 and Red 2. Smith anticipated a

163 Ibid., 186–90.

164 Ibid., 193.

tough fight against the estimated 1,000 Japanese defenders still on the island.[165]

Marines led by First Lieutenant Alexander "Sandy" Bonnyman storming the final Japanese stronghold on Betio (National Archives 532517).

The Japanese counterattack finally came on the third night of the operation. The Marines had anticipated this and had prepared a defense with integrated direct fires, mortars, field artillery, and naval gunfire support. A series of four Japanese attacks commenced at 1930 against the American lines east of Red 3. The final and most serious attack came against two companies of the 8th Marines, when up to 400 Japanese troops rushed their positions at 0400. Though the Marines suffered heavy casualties, they repulsed every attack. The fire support provided by their field artillery—a single battalion fired 1,300 75-mm rounds over the course

165 Ibid., 197–98.

of the night—and the destroyers *Schroeder* (DD-501) and *Sigsbee* (DD-502) were crucial to the American defense. Both destroyers emptied their magazines of 5-inch shells during the action, and *Schroeder*'s constant firing popped rivets from her after deckhouse and caused the accidental launch of a depth charge. "Those destroyers saved our lives," concluded one Marine sergeant.[166]

The fighting on the night of 22–23 November dramatically altered the combat power ratio on Betio, with at least 400 Japanese troops killed in the fighting.[167] The Marines continued their attacks the next morning against rapidly deteriorating Japanese resistance, simultaneously reaching the eastern end of the island and clearing the stubborn positions around Red 1 at approximately 1300.[168] Julian Smith finally declared the end of organized resistance on Betio at 1305 on 23 November, nearly 76 hours after the first Marine landings.[169] The tiny island's seizure had cost 1,027 American lives.[170] Only 17 Japanese troops and 129 Korean laborers survived the fighting.[171] Even before the firing stopped, Seabees were busy at work repairing Betio's airstrip in preparation for subsequent operations.[172]

BUTARITARI LANDINGS

One-hundred and thirty-six miles north of Betio, operations to seize Makin Atoll commenced at 0610 on 20 November with an aerial bombardment of Butaritari Island. Naval gunfire initiated at 0640 and continued until 0824. The first of two major loss-of-life incidents for the Navy at Makin occurred during this phase when *Mississippi* (BB-41) suffered an explosion in her No. 2 main battery turret, killing 43 officers and men and

166 Ibid., 198–201.

167 Ibid., 201.

168 Ibid., 202, 204–205.

169 Alexander, *Across the Reef*, 46.

170 Shaw, Nalty, and Turnbladh, *Central Pacific Drive*, 636.

171 Alexander, *Across the Reef*, 46.

172 Alexander, *Utmost Savagery*, 205.

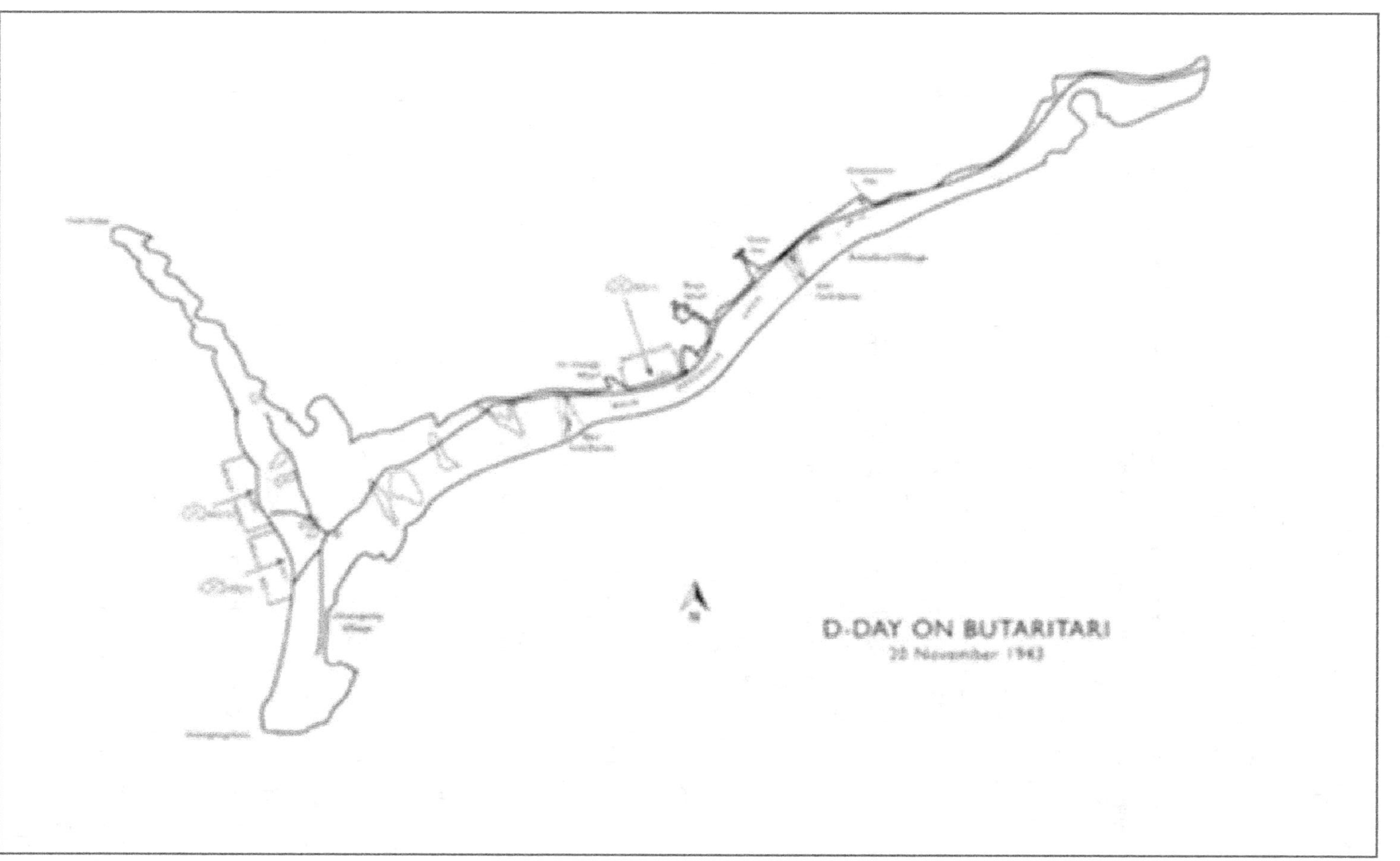
D-DAY ON BUTARITARI
20 November 1943

Mississippi (BB-41)

Mississippi was the second battleship named after the state. Her predecessor, BB-23, had been sold to the Greek government in 1914, only six years after her commissioning. *Mississippi* (BB-41) was commissioned on 18 December 1917. In a tragic precedent to her turret accident during Galvanic, 48 crewmembers were asphyxiated when her No. 2 main battery turret suffered an explosion during gunnery practice on 12 June 1924. She was in Iceland protecting shipping in December 1941, thus escaping the Japanese attack at Pearl Harbor. Moving to the Pacific, *Mississippi* spent the first months of the war in training and escorting convoys. She finally saw action on 22 July 1943, when she shelled Kiska Island during the Aleutians campaign.[1]

After the Gilberts invasion, *Mississippi* served through many of the Pacific War's major campaigns. She bombarded Kwajalein, Taroa, and Wotje in the Marshalls in January and, February 1944, moved to the Southwest Pacific and attacked Kavieng, New Ireland, in March. After an overhaul in the Puget Sound, she supported the Peleliu invasion beginning 12 September 1944. The next month, *Mississippi* participated in the invasion of Leyte, Philippines, and the Battle of Surigao Strait, the last naval engagement between battleships, and one of only two such actions in the Pacific War. At Suriago Strait she fired the last salvo in what turned out to be the final battleship duel in naval history.[2]

While supporting the landings at Lingayen Gulf, Philippines, in January 1945, a *kamikaze* aircraft struck her near the waterline. After repairs at Pearl Harbor, *Mississippi* supported the seizure of Okinawa in May–June 1945, where she leveled Shuri Castle, part of

1 "*Mississippi* II (Battleship No. 23)," DANFS, https://www.history.navy.mil/research/histories/ship-histories/danfs/m/mississippi-ii.html, accessed 12 September 2019; "Mississippi III (Battleship No. 41)," DANFS, https://www.history.navy.mil/research/histories/ship-histories/danfs/m/mississippi-iii.html, accessed 12 September 2019.

2 Samuel Eliot Morison, *History of United States Naval Operations in World War II, Volume 12: Leyte, June 1944–January 1945* (Boston: Little, Brown and Company, 1958), 224, 226.

wounding 19.[173] Destroyers *Phelps* (DD-360) and *Macdonough* (DD-351) marked the line of departure as the first waves of troops moved toward the beaches in LVTs.[174]

As they approached the Red beaches, the LVTs commenced firing with machine guns and specially designed rockets. Many of the rockets

173 "USS MISSISSIPPI—Act Rep, bombardment of Makin Atoll, 11/20/43," World War II War Diaries.

174 Morison, *Aleutians, Gilberts, and Marshalls*, 124–25.

a defensive complex that had held up the entire U.S. Tenth Army advance. She suffered another suicide plane attack on 5 June, but continued to support Allied forces until 16 June. In August 1945, she anchored in Tokyo Bay and witnessed the Japanese surrender. *Mississippi* received eight battle stars for her service in World War II.[3]

Mississippi **(BB-41) in camouflage and underway in Puget Sound, Washington, 13 July 1944. She received eight battle stars for her service in World War II (NHHC NH 104835).**

3 "*Mississippi* II (Battleship No. 23)," DANFS,

landed short, however, or failed to fire due to exposure to salt water.[175] Fortunately, the landings faced virtually no opposition at the Red beaches and the first LVTs touched down at 0832. Elements of two infantry battalions rapidly put ashore.[176] However, follow-on waves found the beaches clogged and difficult to access due to a multitude of coral boulders that created a natural obstacle for LCVPs. These problems delayed the com-

175 Crowl and Love, *Seizure of the Gilberts and the Marshalls*, 77.

176 Ibid., 125.

pletion of the planned landings at the Red beaches for one to two hours.[177] Beach conditions continued to delay logistical operations throughout the day. In sum, only 31 of 250 LCVP loads and 18 of 28 LCM loads got ashore on the Red beaches on D-Day.[178] Nonetheless, by 1100 the troops had secured a limit of advance 1,300 yards inland from the western beaches.[179]

At 1041, another battalion began landing at the Yellow beaches, with minesweeper *Revenge* (AM-110) and destroyers *Phelps* and *Macdonough* clearing the route into the lagoon and providing close bombardment. The LVT-mounted rockets proved very effective in supporting the landings in this sector. Troops at the Yellow beaches faced some enemy fire but overall opposition was light. Japanese troops had occupied several hulks on the western end of Yellow 1, and they attempted to enfilade American troops as they landed. Machine guns from an LCVP, then aerial bombing, and finally *Dewey*'s (DD-349) 5-inch guns all engaged these positions over the course of several hours, but in doing so they nearly hit American troops and slowed down the landing operations.[180]

Despite the logistical difficulties experienced in the landings, the 165th RCT overcame most enemy positions from the western beaches to the main fortified area between the tank barriers by the close of D-day. Japanese resistance was generally light on D-day, though a sniper killed Colonel Gardiner Conroy, the regiment's commander.[181] Major General Ralph Smith was ashore by 1800 on D-day.[182] With the exception of *Minneapolis* (CA-36), *Dewey*, and *Phelps*, all combatant ships retired in the late afternoon to join the Northern Carrier Group.[183] The troops

---

177 Crowl and Love, *Seizure of the Gilberts and the Marshalls*, 78–79, 82.

178 Morison, *Aleutians, Gilberts, and Marshalls*, 125.

179 Crowl and Love, *Seizure of the Gilberts and the Marshalls*, 82.

180 Ibid., 83–88.

181 Ibid., 97.

182 Ibid., 106.

183 Ibid., 105; Morison, *Aleutians, Gilberts and Marshalls*, 133.

ashore issued no calls for naval gunfire or close air support on the first day.[184]

Smith and his superiors might have anticipated a quick finishing of the job against a vastly outnumbered Japanese force, but the 27th Infantry Division failed to sustain its initial steady progress on Butaritari. A series of frustrating and tragicomic incidents marked the second day on the island. The first task of the day was the reduction of Japanese pockets of resistance around the western tank barrier. This action was complete by late morning, but a fratricide incident marred the operation when a Navy bomber dropped a 2,000-pound bomb on a group of tanks, killing three U.S. soldiers. On the Yellow beaches, a variety of landing craft, tanks, and aircraft spent much of the day attacking the hulks on the western edge of the landing area due to suspected Japanese firing. A dismounted patrol finally investigated the hulks and found no evidence of Japanese activity on them. The firing in the lagoon delayed the landing of supplies for much of the day.[185] By the end of the second day, the American front lines lay just west of the eastern tank barrier. The troops had cleared the main defensive positions on the island, but they had advanced less than a mile while incurring even fewer casualties than on D-day.[186]

"Howlin' Mad" Smith was furious at the Army's slow progress and came ashore to assess the situation. Smith's opinion was that the island "should have been secured by dusk on D-Day" and that "any Marine regiment would have done it in that time." This judgment, his conclusion that "the 165th was not too well officered," and his near wounding that night at the hands of nervous sentries all contributed to a major rift between Smith and Army leadership that would explode in later operations.[187]

By the evening of the third day on Butaritari, American forces had pushed past the eastern tank trap and about halfway up the eastern end of

---

184 Crowl and Love, *Seizure of the Gilberts and the Marshalls*, 105.

185 Ibid., 109–11.

186 Ibid., 116.

187 Holland M. Smith and Percy Finch, *Coral and Brass* (New York: Charles Scribner's Sons, 1949), 125–28.

the island. As at Betio, the Japanese finally mounted a counterattack that night, inflicting light casualties at a cost of more than 50 killed. The 165th RCT pushed through sporadic resistance and reached the eastern end of the island the next morning around 1030. Ralph Smith reported "Makin taken" to Admiral Turner shortly before Julian Smith's similar report from Betio. Including 105 prisoners, all but one of whom were Korean laborers, Japanese casualties numbered around 550. Army casualties consisted of 66 killed or died of wounds and 152 wounded in action.[188]

JAPANESE COUNTERATTACK

Even with the limited forces available to Admiral Koga, the fears of Nimitz and other Navy leaders were somewhat vindicated by a series of limited attacks on the American fleet. On the evening of 20 November, 16 torpedo bombers attacked the Southern Carrier Group off Tarawa. Antiaircraft fire splashed eight of the planes, but six managed to close on *Independence* and drop at least five torpedoes. One torpedo struck the carrier, killing 17 sailors, wounding 43, and causing damage significant enough to force her to withdraw to Funafati for repairs. Fortunately, this attack and a few insignificant bombing raids on Betio constituted the total damage inflicted by Japanese air power during the ground combat phase of Galvanic.[189]

Koga had also dispatched submarines to the Gilberts, the first of which, *I-35*, arrived off Tarawa on 22 November. *Meade* (DD-602) picked up the contact and began a series of depth-charge attacks along with *Frazier*. The submarine hunt culminated when *Frazier* rammed the boat and then used small-arms fire to prevent the crew from manning their deck guns. *Frazier* captured only two surviving Japanese sailors from the sunken boat.[190]

The slow pace of operations on Butaritari had much deadlier consequences for the naval forces supporting the landings. Early on the morning

188 Crowl and Love, *Seizure of the Gilberts and the Marshalls*, 123–25.

189 Morison, *Aleutians, Gilberts and Marshalls*, 138, 141.

190 Ibid., 139; "USS FRAZIER—War Diary, 11/1-30/43," 330, World War II War Diaries.

of 24 November, *I-175* approached the escort carriers *Liscome Bay* (CVE-56), *Coral Sea* (CVE-57), and *Corregidor* (CVE-58) 20 miles southwest of Makin Atoll. The submarine managed to slip through the destroyer screen and sighted *Liscome Bay* broadside at first light. Lieutenant Commander Tadashi Tabata fired a torpedo spread, and a single torpedo struck the carrier amidships at about 0510. A series of spectacular explosions followed, demolishing the aft third of the vessel and scattering debris on American ships nearly a mile away. The ship sank in 23 minutes. Burning fuel covered the water as destroyers *Morris* (DD-417) and *Hughes* (DD-410) moved in to rescue survivors. A final tally revealed 644 officers and men killed in action, including *Liscome Bay*'s Captain Irving D. Wiltsie, Rear Admiral Henry M. Mullinnix, and Cook Third Class Doris "Dorie" Miller, who had previously become the first African American recipient of the Navy Cross for his actions in combat at Pearl Harbor. Fifty-five officers and 217 men survived.[191] *I-175* fired at another escort carrier and missed, then withdrew unharmed.[192]

Sixty-eight planes had reinforced Koga's forces by 25 November. That evening thirteen Japanese bombers attacked elements of the Northern Attack Force about sixty miles east of Butaritari. Under the command of Rear Admiral Turner, the group carefully observed the synchronization of Japanese floating lights and parachute flairs and executed a series of coordinated turns. These evasive maneuvers thwarted Japanese attempts to strike the group, resulting in no ships lost or damaged. The constant drills executed on the movement from Pearl Harbor to Makin had paid off.[193]

On the same evening, Japanese planes attacked the Northern Carrier Group under Rear Admiral Radford. In response to a pattern of Japanese night attacks, famed Medal of Honor recipient Lieutenant Commander

191 Morison, *Aleutians, Gilberts and Marshalls*, 140–41; "Naval Profiles—Miller, Doris," Naval History and Heritage Command, https://www.history.navy.mil/content/history/nhhc/research/histories/biographies-list/bios-m/miller-doris.html, accessed 29 August 2019.

192 Morison, *Aleutians, Gilberts and Marshalls*, 141.

193 Ibid., 142–43.

Edward H. "Butch" O'Hare

"Butch" O'Hare was one of the United States' first heroes of World War II. After graduation from the Naval Academy in 1937, O'Hare served on *New Mexico* (BB-40) for two years before reporting for flight training at Naval Air Station Pensacola, Florida.[1] On 20 February 1942, Lieutenant O'Hare was an aviator assigned to VF-3 on *Lexington* (CV-2). On that day, after an aborted attempt to strike the Japanese base at Rabaul, *Lexington* came under attack by eight Japanese bombers. Due to a prior enemy bomber attack and the subsequent timing of launch and recovery operations, O'Hare and another officer piloted the only fighter aircraft on hand to provide cover for the carrier as the Japanese bombers approached. With his wingman's guns failing to fire, O'Hare single-handedly attacked the eight bombers. He received credit for downing five of them in four minutes of action to become the first American flying ace of the war. The bombers that escaped failed to strike any American ship. For his actions in defense of *Lexington*, O'Hare received the Medal of Honor at a White House ceremony in April 1942.[2]

After touring the nation to encourage war bond purchases, O'Hare assumed command of VF-3 in June 1942.[3] O'Hare led the squadron, redesignated VF-6, back into combat in August and September 1943 in raids on Marcus and Wake islands. For his actions in these operations, including two more downed Japanese aircraft at Wake Island, O'Hare would later receive the Distinguished Flying Cross and a gold star in lieu of a second award.[4]

O'Hare assumed command of Carrier Air Group Six (CAG-6) on 13 October 1943, and would lead that unit in Operation Galvanic. A tactical expert and innovator, O'Hare had helped his former squadron commander John S. "Jimmy" Thach work out the famed "Thach weave" maneuver in 1941, and he took a leading role in developing night-fighting tactics while on *Enterprise*.[5] O'Hare was also a "flying CAG," who led from the front and personally experimented with tactics and techniques while training his pilots. Characteristically, he chose to fly in one of the two night-fighting teams he had created, participating in the first-ever attempted night-intercept operation on 24 November 1943.[6] Returning empty-handed, he flew again on the successful mission of 26 November. O'Hare posthumously received the Navy Cross for his role in this historic combat action.[7]

Today, O'Hare's name is familiar to the millions of people who pass through Chicago O'Hare International Airport. A native of St. Louis, Missouri, O'Hare's connection to the Windy City during his life came via his father Edgar J. "EJ" O'Hare, a lawyer and businessman with dealings in Chicago. The elder O'Hare was at one time associated with the infa-

1 Steve Ewing and John B. Lundstrom, *Fateful Rendezvous: The Life of Butch O'Hare* (Annapolis, MD: Naval Institute Press, 1997), 58–60, 65–70.
2 Ewing and Lundstrom, *Fateful Rendezvous*, 124–40.
3 Ewing and Lundstrom, *Fateful Rendezvous*, 150–66.
4 Ibid., 197–17.
5 Ibid., 104–105, 241–51.
6 Ibid., 252–54.
7 Ibid., 287–94.

mous Al Capone but he became an informant for the federal government and testified against Capone in the 1931 trial that sent the gangster to prison. Assassins murdered EJ O'Hare in Chicago in November 1939, shortly before Capone's release from prison. After the war, *Chicago Tribune* editor and publisher Robert T. McCormick suggested that the city should rename its new airport in Butch O'Hare's honor. A campaign led by the Naval Airmen of America, a veteran's organization, ultimately led to the dedication of the airport to O'Hare's memory on 18 September 1949.[8]

Lieutenant Edward H. Butch O'Hare, USN, taken on 10 April 1942 at Naval Air Station, Maui, Hawaii, in the cockpit of his Grumman F4F-3 Wildcat fighter. O'Hare received the Medal of Honor for shooting down five Japanese planes on 20 February 1942 while defending *Lexington* (CV-3) (NHHC 80-G-10562).

8 Ewing and Lundstrom, *Fateful Rendezvous*, 27–38, 76–80, 303–304.

Edward H. "Butch" O'Hare, air group commander on *Enterprise* (CV-6), and Lieutenant Commander John L. Phillips, commander of torpedo squadron VT-6, had previously created two improvised night-fighting teams. These teams each used one radar-equipped Grumman TBF Avenger and two standard Grumman F6F Hellcats to provide an improvised night-fighting capability. As the enemy planes drew near, *Enterprise* launched the first team, which included O'Hare and Phillips. Using the ship's radar and that of the *Avenger*, Phillips surprised and shot down two Japanese bombers. Unfortunately, the team had separated before the shooting began. As they attempted to rendezvous, a Japanese bomber materialized on O'Hare's tail and opened fire, killing the famed aviator. The Japanese attackers failed to strike any of the American ships. Though the fleet would mourn the loss of the popular O'Hare, this action marked the first successful night intercept by carrier-based aviation.[194]

During the same evening, *Radford* (DD-446) sank another Japanese submarine while screening the Northern Carrier Group and a group of Bettys attacked the Relief Carrier Group on the evening of 28 November. The Japanese lost more planes in the attack and failed once again to inflict any damage on American ships. With this action, Koga's *Hei* No. 3 operation sputtered to a close.[195]

As November 1943 ended, most American carriers were withdrawn from the Gilberts. With the exception of *Independence*'s damage and *Liscome Bay*'s destruction, the Japanese naval and air response to the American invasion had been toothless. Only 47 American aircraft had been lost in combat out of 73 operational losses, and despite its human cost, the sinking of *Liscome Bay* had done nothing to stop the American invasion. As for the Japanese, they had incurred heavy losses once again,

194 Ibid., 143; Steve Ewing and John B. Lundstrom, *Fateful Rendezvous: The Life of Butch O'Hare* (Annapolis, MD: Naval Institute Press, 1997), 214–54, 273–86.

195 Morison, *Aleutians, Gilberts and Marshalls*, 144.

suffering more than 100 aircraft and at least three submarines lost during Galvanic.[196]

MOPPING UP

While Fifth Fleet was parrying Koga's thrusts at sea, the Marines were completing the seizure of Apamama and Tarawa atolls. The V Amphibious Corps Reconnaissance Company was to reconnoiter Apamama and seize it if possible on the night of 19–20 November. *Nautilus* was to deliver the unit by rubber boat, but while on the surface en route to the objective *Ringgold* mistook her for an enemy submarine and opened fire, striking her conning tower with a 5-inch shell and forcing her to dive. Fortunately, the shell failed to explode and the crew made repairs once it was safe to surface. *Nautilus* finally arrived off Apamama on the afternoon of 20 November, and the Marines began movement to one of the islands in the predawn hours of 21 November. A minor skirmish with a Japanese patrol marked the action on the first day of the operation, but the Marines encountered more resistance on an island to the northeast, code-named "Otto." A platoon-sized element on Otto held off the Marines on 23 November despite shelling from *Nautilus*. The following day, a destroyer arrived and fired on the Japanese, killing four and prompting the rest to commit suicide. Marine garrison forces assumed control of Apamama that afternoon.[197]

Meanwhile at Tarawa, some Japanese troops had escaped the fighting on Betio and retreated to the northern reaches of the atoll. LT 2/6 received the mission of clearing Japanese forces from the remainder of Tarawa.

---

196 Morison, *Aleutians, Gilberts and Marshalls*, 144–45. Sources disagree on the identities and timelines of the loss of several Japanese submarines during this period. See Morison, *Aleutians, Gilberts and Marshalls*; Office of the Chief of Naval Operations, *German, Japanese, and Italian Submarine Losses: World War II* (Washington, DC: Office of the Chief of Naval Operations, 1946), 23; Dorr Carpenter and Norman Polmar, *Submarines of the Imperial Japanese Navy* (Annapolis, MD: United States Naval Institute Press, 1986), 36.

197 Shaw, Nalty, and Turnbladh, *Central Pacific Drive*, 102.

The battalion pushed across the many islands of the atoll, encountering no Japanese until the late afternoon of 26 November, when Marine and Japanese patrols collided in a small skirmish. Advancing the next morning, the Marines found the Japanese dug in within an area of thick cover on the island of Buariki. The poor visibility and close range of the fighting hampered the use of artillery support and the Marines overran the enemy positions in vicious infantry fighting. By the end of the day on 27 November, the battle of Buariki was over, having cost 32 dead and 59 wounded Marines in exchange for 175 Japanese killed and two captured. The following morning, the Marines pushed to the end of Naa Island, marking the extreme northern end of Tarawa Atoll. The entire atoll was finally in American hands, ending Operation Galvanic.[198]

GALVANIC'S LESSONS

For many Americans, the casualties suffered in Galvanic were shocking and seemed out of proportion to the importance of possessing a few small coral atolls in the Central Pacific. For years, many would debate the necessity of Galvanic and the competency of its execution. In his memoir, Holland Smith famously concluded, "Tarawa was a mistake."[199]

With the exception of Vice Admiral Towers, a vocal partisan for the capabilities of carrier aviation, none of Smith's peers agreed with this assessment.[200] The lessons learned in the Gilberts were numerous and crucial to future successes in the Central Pacific drive. Though some aspects of the operation had clearly worked well—the use of LVTs to cross the reefs, the landing of field artillery on Bairiki, LVT-mounted rockets, and close gunfire support by destroyers—much of the operation had been plagued with difficulties.[201] In the battle's immediate aftermath, the 2nd Marine Division created a list of 14 specific recommendations focused on

198 Ibid., 98.

199 Smith and Finch, *Coral and Brass*, 134.

200 Reynolds, *Admiral John H. Towers*, 439; Buell, *The Quiet Warrior*, 272; Dyer, *The Amphibians Came to Conquer*, 728–30; Alexander, *Utmost Savagery*, 243.

201 Crowl and Love, *Seizure of the Gilberts and Marshalls*, 161.

the execution of amphibious doctrine and preparation, organization, and equipage for amphibious assault, and sent them up the chain of command.[202] Likewise, Vice Admiral Turner forwarded to Pearl Harbor a paper entitled "Lessons Learned at Tarawa" that directly affected planning for the invasion of the Marshalls.[203]

Photographed in March 1944 by Lieutenant Commander Charles Kerlee, USNR, a wrecked Japanese tank and three U.S. Marine LVT-1 amphibious vehicles still litter a Betio beach, where they were destroyed in battle on 20–23 November 1943 (NHHC 80-G-401620).

202 Alexander, *Utmost Savagery*, 235.

203 Morison, *Aleutians, Gilberts and Marshalls*, 202–203.

The Navy and ground forces had learned much about naval gunfire and close air support, both of which had been less than effective during the operation. Instead of neutralization fire over a wide area, fire-support groups had to pinpoint enemy positions and adjust fire until they achieved destruction. Whereas naval gunfire tactics had previously called for ships maneuvering evasively and firing at long ranges against enemy coastal artillery, Betio demonstrated that destroying hardened positions required sustained, close-range engagement with armor-piercing shells. Fire-support plans also had to be conditions-based, rather than set to a timetable in order to avoid the disastrous early lifting of fires as had occurred at Betio.[204]

Northwestern end of Betio Island, Tarawa, 22 November 1943. Beach Red 1 is on the left and Green beach is in the center and right (NHHC NH 95704).

204 Donald M. Weller, "Salvo—Splash! Part I: The Development of Naval Gunfire Support in World War II," *Proceedings* (August 1954): 849.

Several adaptations mitigated these problems in future operations. For instance, spotting planes would facilitate tracking of the front-line trace of assault forces.[205] In recognition of the fact that "effective gunfire support required a thorough knowledge of the gunnery problem," Joint Assault Signal Companies replaced provisional shore fire-control parties, with specially trained fire-control parties established at echelons from battalion to division. Additionally, acquisition of Kahoolawee in the Hawaiian Islands in late September 1943 gave the Pacific Fleet a bombardment range to train its gunnery crews in shore bombardment for future operations.[206]

Throughout the fighting on Betio and Butaritari, carrier aircraft bombed and strafed Japanese positions in an attempt to support the ground troops. Unfortunately, air-ground coordination was a continual problem and American aircraft inadvertently targeted friendly forces in more than one instance. Overall, the Marines were especially unimpressed with the effectiveness of naval aviation during the battle for Betio.[207] Among their recommendations were additional training between amphibious forces and supporting carrier aircraft, ideally with Marine aviators in support of Marine divisions in the future. In short, Navy pilots required careful indoctrination in close air support tactics. Air space clearance was another area that demanded improvement. Rather than segregating air and naval bombardment by time and zone, they could overlap so long as dive-bombers stayed above the maximum ordinate for naval guns. As with naval gunfire, aviation units supporting landing forces should base their attacks on the actual distance of troops from the beaches rather than on a timeline relative to H-hour.[208]

The Marines and Army also demanded better equipment. In light of the rampant communications problems they had suffered, more effective

205 Ibid.

206 Donald M. Weller, "Salvo—Splash! Part II: The Development of Naval Gunfire Support in World War II," *Proceedings* (September 1954): 1017–18.

207 Ibid., 122–23, 132; Alexander, *Across the Reef*, 30.

208 Shaw, Nalty, and Turnbladh, *Central Pacific Drive*, 113–14.

and waterproofed radios were a necessity. Julian and Ralph Smith also deemed amphibian tractors indispensable, with Julian Smith recommending no less than 300 of them per Marine division. They recommended upgraded models with factory-installed armor, stronger engines, more and better weapons, drop ramps, and variants with turret-mounted weapons. These recommendations would manifest themselves in the large numbers of LVT-4s and LVT(A)-4s on hand seven months later for the Marianas operations.[209] The Marines also desired more firepower: the use of Sherman medium tanks only; more flamethrowers with a higher fuel capacity and large, tank-mounted flamethrowers; bunker-buster bombs designed to kill the enemy with the effects of the blast wave; and more tractors with mounted rockets to support the final approach to the beach.[210]

Several issues in ship-to-shore operations spurred improvements in future campaigns. In spite of the Army's issues at Butaritari, after-action reports lauded the 27th Infantry Division's efficient use of palletized supplies, in contrast to the Marines' manhandling of equipment and supplies at Betio. Both forces learned that load plans had to put ashore equipment and supplies in accordance with the current phase of the operation. To better control supply operations, a naval officer at the line of departure would command boats tasked to control and direct traffic to and from the beachhead.[211] In the future, rather than relying on the limited capabilities of aid stations ashore and ships' sick bays, reviews suggested that hospital ships be assigned to task forces charged with seizing heavily defended atolls.[212] Perhaps the most frustrating issue of all for Hill, Turner, and other commanders had been the poor quality of radio communications resulting from makeshift and unreliable command suites rigged aboard

---

209 Shaw, Nalty, and Turnbladh, *Central Pacific Drive*, 107–108; Alexander, *Utmost Savagery*, 233–34; Crowl and Love, *Seizure of the Gilberts and Marshalls*, 164–65.

210 Alexander, *Utmost Savagery*, 236–37; Crowl and Love, *Seizure of the Gilberts and Marshalls*, 161.

211 Crowl and Love, *Seizure of the Gilberts and Marshalls*, 163–64.

212 Shaw, Nalty, and Turnbladh, *Central Pacific Drive*, 112.

combatant ships. The Navy would use dedicated amphibious command ships in future operations.[213]

Finally, the Navy's ignorance of beach conditions and inability to deal with shallow water obstacles during the operation were causes for concern. A post-battle examination of Betio revealed that the landings fortunately took place in the only part of the island that lacked mines, with 3,000 mines found ashore that the Japanese had yet to emplace in the lagoon. Highlighting this danger, mines had quickly destroyed two LVTs that had strayed from the cleared approaches during the fighting. The conditions at the Red beaches at Butaritari also exposed problems with pre-landing reconnaissance. The Navy, especially Rear Admiral Turner, recognized the need for specially trained swimmers for reconnaissance and demolition work in future operations and pushed for the development of Underwater Demolition Teams.[214] The Army and Navy had already been at work on this program for several months, but Turner urged its rapid expansion in light of his experiences during Galvanic. With the backing of Admiral Nimitz, the Navy quickly established a school in Hawaii to train what would become UDT 1 and UDT 2. The seizure of Kwajalein in January 1944 would mark the first combat deployment of Navy UDTs.[215]

SUMMARY AND ANALYSIS

Operation Galvanic demonstrated for the first time in the Pacific War the United States' ability to move a large, self-sustaining invasion force across thousands of miles of ocean and successfully assault a fortified and strongly defended island. Fearful of a potential attack by the Japanese Combined Fleet based in the Marshall Islands, U.S. plans called for a rapid seizure of Betio and Makin Atolls to limit the exposure of Turner's fleet. This emphasis unfortunately resulted in a curtailed and ineffective pre-landing bombardment and an inadvertent misallocation of resources

213 Ibid., 107–108.

214 Dyer, *Amphibians Came to Conquer*, 681.

215 Francis D. Fane, *The Naked Warriors* (Annapolis, MD: Naval Institute Press, 1995), 13, 24–25, 28–29.

between the two objectives. Combined with a lack of experience with amphibious operations, uncertain hydrographic information, and a limited understanding of Japanese capabilities and tactics, the result was a costly 76 hours of combat at Betio before the island was under American control.

On the more exposed northern flank of the operation, the 27th Infantry Division had the equipment, troop strength, and naval gunfire and air support to seize Butaritari quickly and limit the fleet's vulnerability to counterattack. Yet the division's performance was disappointing, with the 165th RCT taking nearly as long to clear the island of Japanese resistance as the Marines did on the much more strongly defended Betio. The slow pace of operations on the island placed the ships of the Northern Task Force in danger, with the carriers still standing by to cover the task force's withdrawal at the time of *Liscome Bay*'s sinking. Turner's fleet was fortunate in that beyond this one incident, the Japanese were virtually powerless to launch a counterattack in the Gilberts due to their earlier losses in the northern Solomons. At Galvanic's conclusion, the United States had established a lodgment in the Japanese perimeter to be exploited in subsequent operations.

Galvanic's contribution to victory in the Pacific was not limited to lessons bloodily learned. The base at Pearl Harbor was finally secure, and the Japanese now confronted a dilemma in countering a two-pronged American advance in the Pacific.[216] By mid-December 1943, American planes were operating out of an airfield at Makin, and three other airfields in the Gilberts were operational by mid-January 1944. Heavy and medium bombers from the Gilberts mounted hundreds of sorties against the Marshalls in support of the upcoming Operation Flintlock. The new airfields also enabled photoreconnaissance of objectives in the Marshalls, crucial to amphibious operations.[217]

Flintlock and its follow-on operation, Catchpole, inflicted approximately 11,000 Japanese casualties and seized control of the Marshalls at a

216 Alexander, *Utmost Savagery*, 242–243.

217 Crowl and Love, *Seizure of the Gilberts and Marshalls*, 157–58.

cost of around 600 American deaths.[218] At no time in the operation were American forces close to repulse as at Betio. By the conclusion of Galvanic and Flintlock, the United States had achieved a 1,000-mile penetration of the Japanese outer defensive perimeter established in 1942, and greatly accelerated the timeline for subsequent operations in the Central Pacific drive.[219]

The seizure of Tarawa and Makin was an inelegant, costly operation replete with mistakes in training, tactics, planning, and leadership. Yet Galvanic seems to have been an unavoidable first step in what became the decisive campaign of the Pacific War. The many soldiers, sailors, and Marines who died signaled to the American public a new phase of the war with Japan, girding the nation for a fight to the finish. American control of the Gilberts set the stage for Operation Flintlock and the long march to victory in the Pacific. Perhaps most importantly, the lessons learned from the operation reaped immediate dividends in the advance into the Marshall Islands, and laid the foundation for the amphibious operations that became characteristic of the United States' war in the Pacific.

---

218 Ibid., 301, 331, 365.

219 Ibid., 372–74; Joseph Alexander, *Storm Landings: Epic Amphibious Battles in the Central Pacific* (Annapolis, MD: Naval Institute Press, 1997), 61.

FURTHER READING

Alexander, Joseph H. *Across the Reef: The Marine Assault on Tarawa.* Washington, DC: Marine Corps Historical Center, 1993.

———. Utmost Savagery: *The Three Days of Tarawa.* Annapolis, MD: Naval Institute Press, 1995.

———. *Storm Landings: Epic Amphibious Battles in the Central Pacific.* Annapolis, MD: Naval Institute Press, 1997.

Crowl, Philip A., and Edmund G. Love. *United States Army in World War II: The War in the Pacific—Seizure of the Gilberts and Marshalls.* Washington, DC: Department of the Army, 1955.

Dyer, George C. *The Amphibians Came to Conquer, Volume 2.* Washington, DC: Government Printing Office, 1972.

Morison, Samuel Eliot. *History of United States Naval Operations in World War II, Volume VII: Aleutians, Gilberts and Marshalls, June 1942–April 1944.* Boston: Little, Brown and Company, 1951.

Shaw, Henry I., Jr., Bernard C. Nalty, and Edwin T. Trumbladh. *History of U.S. Marine Corps Operations in World War II, Volume 3: Central Pacific Drive.* Washington, DC: Historical Branch, U.S. Marine Corps, 1966.

Smith, Holland M., and Percy Finch. *Coral and Brass.* New York: Charles Scribner's Sons, 1949.

Toll, Ian W. *The Conquering Tide: War in the Pacific Islands, 1942–1944.* New York: W. W. Norton & Company, 2015.

ABOUT THE AUTHORS

S. Matthew Cheser holds an M.A. from the University of Maryland–College Park and worked for four years as a historian at Naval History and Heritage Command. He currently serves as a historian at the Defense POW/MIA Accounting Agency.

Nicholas Roland is a U.S. Army veteran and holds a Ph.D. from the University of Texas at Austin. His first book, *Violence in the Hill Country: The Texas Frontier in the Civil War Era*, is forthcoming from University of Texas Press.

www.ingramcontent.com/pod-product-compliance
Lightning Source LLC
LaVergne TN
LVHW061225100826
845148LV00004B/864

* 9 7 8 1 8 3 9 3 1 5 1 1 4 *